> gaze on this leav...
what should be
be forgot ... then
burn like the sun, ...
should be burned. WSR

Wallace Stevens:
An Anatomy of Figuration

WALLACE STEVENS:

An Anatomy of Figuration

By

Eugene Paul Nassar

Philadelphia
University of Pennsylvania Press

To my Mother

and

the memory of my Father

Preface

This essay is intended as a contribution to the body of knowledge about Stevens' poems that will enable critics of the next decade or so to come to a clearer understanding, and more balanced view of Stevens than that which we have now. I have tried to let Stevens speak for himself and keep my own beliefs and attitudes out of the essay as much as possible. The primary purpose of my effort is to explicate, not to criticize, but this is not to say that I have been able to keep all of my opinions on the poems to myself, or that I find Stevens a completely impeccable poet. It is my hope that with proper use of the two Indexes in the Appendix and attention to the cross-references throughout, the reader will find this book a useful guide to detail in Stevens' poems. The analyses are condensed, and should be read with the poetical texts at hand. I have worked without the benefit of a Stevens' concordance, but one has now appeared and can serve to check my discussions of figures here. I have used the abbreviations C.P., O.P., and N.A. for *Collected Poems*, *Opus Posthumous*, and *The Necessary Angel*, respectively.

I am grateful to the Estate of Wallace Stevens and to Alfred A. Knopf, Inc., the publisher of the poetry of Wallace Stevens, for permitting me to reprint from the following copyrighted editions: *The Collected Poems of Wallace Stevens* (1954), and *Opus Posthumous* (1957).

And of course one's obligations to one's teachers never end. Professors Charles Coffin, John Crowe Ransom and Denham Sutcliffe at Kenyon College, and Christopher Ricks at Worcester College, Oxford, among so many others, have contributed to my critical approaches in ways too hard to segregate.

GENE NASSAR

Utica College of Syracuse University.

NOTE TO THE SECOND PRINTING

Stevens has been much written about in the three years since this book went to press, but the poems, I feel, continue to be often handled with inaccurate response to tone (Stevens as a romantic or transcendentalist) and imprecision concerning local detail. The most important addition to the Stevens literature is the edition of the *Letters* (ed. Holly Stevens, New York, 1966). I have gone through the letters and have found that in matters of general attitude and in local figuration, I need regret little or nothing in my original text so far as Stevens' intentions are concerned. I might now use statements from the letters to grace my approach but surely one ought not to do so, for, as Stevens says in a letter, "The final authority is the poem itself" (p. 390). I would refer the critical reader to the letters of Stevens to, say, Harriet Monroe, Ronald Lane Latimer, Hi Simons, and Henry Church, and to the citations in the Index to the *Letters* of specific Stevens poems. I have in the present text made only a few typographical and word changes.

E.P.N.
February, 1968

Contents

PART ONE

An Anatomy of Specific Figures

Chapter One

The Two Minds of Wallace Stevens

As if, as if, as if the disparate halves
Of things were waiting in a betrothal known
To none, awaiting espousal to the sound
Of right joining, a music of ideas, the burning
And breeding and bearing birth of harmony,
The final relation, the marriage of the rest. (C.P. 464–5)

In that final task of the critic, the groping for the true
tonality, the actual complex of emotions of which the poet
writes, Wallace Stevens has given his critics more than the
usual amount of trouble. I take it as the common experience
in reading Stevens that one first finds a surface incredibly
bizarre and seemingly impenetrable. Later, in the wish for
simple coherence, the critic is tempted to look at Stevens'
figures as an assemblage of counters in a rather abstract,
doctrinal scheme. However, when the serious critic examines
these figures more closely, he is aware of aspects of them
which consistently undercut, in a conscious, ironic fashion,
the doctrinal substance which other aspects of them are
intended to bear. The critic is disturbed by this oddness
implicit in the figures and in the troubled surface of a given
poem as a whole. The oddness is not really like that of other
modern poets he has studied, if only by virtue of its constant
presence, its diffusion into all areas of Stevens' figuration.

Structural frameworks, embedded stanzas, phrases, or single words all partake of an unfailing double vision that appears to be the very essence of Stevens' mental and emotional life. It will be the purpose of this study to investigate the double nature of Stevens' figures while being as precise as possible in defining the core signification of the "disparate halves" of a specific figure by means of quotation from the texts of the significant appearances of that figure. This effort, so circumscribed, will have the failings of all anatomies: the wider suggestiveness of some of the figures will not be treated. I make no apology for this since I trust one profits from such a study in the same way one does from a musicologist's analysis of a symphonic work.

§ 1   Stevens asserts in his essay, "The Irrational Element in Poetry," "One is always writing about two things at the same time in poetry, and it is this that produces the tension characteristic of poetry. One is the true subject and the other is the poetry of the subject." For Stevens, the true subject was always the object as perceived by the poet, the poetry of the subject is the irrational "distortion" of the object that the imagination performs. Let us look at the two things Stevens is writing about in a poem that has been often looked at as if it meant one thing only.

> I placed a jar in Tennessee,
> And round it was, upon a hill.
> It made the slovenly wilderness
> Surround that hill.
>
> The wilderness rose up to it,
> And sprawled around, no longer wild.
> The jar was round upon the ground
> And tall and of a port in air.

It took dominion everywhere.
The jar was gray and bare.
It did not give of bird or bush,
Like nothing else in Tennessee.   (C.P. 76)

The jar is an object as subject, yet not a natural object but a form created by a man. The poetry of the subject is in the dominion over nature that it has, the power to create an order out of disorder, in both the artist's and the perceiver's mind. (It is one of a cluster of figures of order that Stevens' imagination creates, figures which will be investigated in Chapter Four.) The jar has tamed the "slovenly wilderness," and yet, Stevens would say, since the wilderness *is* slovenly, the jar does violence to the truth of the subject. "The difficulty of sticking to the true subject, when it is the poetry of the subject that is paramount in one's mind, need only be mentioned to be understood." (O.P. 221) The wilderness is certainly no better endured, "sprawled around," held under a false dominion. The real "bird or bush" has been transformed into metaphor. Whether this process gives us something new or simply something false is questionable.

This rather banal statement of the attitudes of the poem is not so important as it is to see that Stevens sees, feels, simultaneously (in this poem as he does everywhere) and reflexively, as it were, both the power and the weakness of an imaginative order.

The jar will also serve as a good introduction to the kind of limiting precision with which Stevens handles his figures. The jar, in context, means two pretty definite things, or, better, one thing seen from two perspectives. It is the art object which, at once, gives a cherished imaginative order to chaos and which, ironically, in imposing a false order on reality, makes life a continual process of lying to oneself.

The jar does not carry with it in this context (a context modified by the whole corpus of Stevens poems on the same essential subject) a trailing load of other associations it could very well have in other contexts. This is not an endlessly reverberating metaphor. In fact, in its doctrinal aspect alone, a Stevens figure is more emblem than symbol.

§ 2   One has only to compare, in their contextual relations, some similar figures from, say, Yeats with those of Stevens to sense the difference between Yeats' expansive and Stevens' limiting way of handling a figure. For example, set side by side Yeats' bird on the golden bough in "Byzantium" with Stevens' red bird in "Le Monocle," Yeats' great-rooted blossomer with the hemlock of "Domination of Black," the swans at Coole with those that have their bills flat upon the ground in "Academic Discourse at Havana." After an acquaintance with Stevens, we come to see that the red bird flies on the scene for two reasons: to revive the aging hero's sense of reality and his mortal condition within it, and to demonstrate, by the brilliant effect it produces in combination with the golden floor, the gaudiness and sensual pleasure the imagination can create from reality. One can explicate in this way with a good deal of confidence, having come to some understanding of the recurrent patterns of Stevens' figures. If one does not have a sense of his patterns, there is really no way of telling what a red bird is doing on a gold floor in this poem at all. The figure is limited by its contextual relations with the whole body of Stevens' poems. Yeats' bird can render itself up to the understanding to a great degree by poring over the pattern of the specific poem. And yet one comes to the realization that the poem has been so designed that the golden bird has a suggestiveness that will evade statement in any precise way. One is never sure whether he is dealing at any given point with myth, aesthetic doctrine, or mystical belief, or, perhaps, with all of these held in balance by a figure that serves the needs of all three. Yeats' figure bears a complex load of signification in itself; Stevens' figure, simpler to understand in itself, is made complex by its being treated ironically in its context. And one would, I think, find the same sort of distinctions between the figures of the trees and the swans.[1] This is not to say that Stevens never deals in an expansive figure, or Yeats in a limited one, but simply that when one sets about to analyze a poem of either man, he looks for complexity to be arrived at in different ways.

§ 3   Stevens abstracts from a given figure something like its (platonic) essence to serve a doctrinal function. For example, though a certain sensibility is offended by the suggestion, it may be asserted that all the various hats in Stevens have pretty much the same signification as something that keeps the sun (or, more generally, the weather) from one's eyes. The sun is Stevens' classic figure for unabstracted reality, and it is not hard to see hats as another evasion in the mind's "motive for metaphor, shrinking from the weight of primary noon." (C.P. 288) The rationalists wear square hats and the imaginative people wear elliptical sombreros. The value judgment implicit in this contrast between straight lines and curved lines will be brought out later (§ 11), but what is essential to notice is that both sorts of people do wear hats. Stevens does not say that it is possible to stand in the sun bareheaded for very long. He believes in the evasions of hats.

A rather tenuous relationship has been established by Stevens between sun and hat, the sun serving as a figure for reality, the hat for the mind's evasion of reality. In such a way, the connection works. However, in most ways of look-

1.   For "Hemlock," see § 38 below; for "Swan," see § 19 and § 39.

ing at these figures, the sun and a hat are comically remote
from any relationship. And Stevens, in fact, often exploits
the possibilities of mixed metaphor, the very real power of
imaginative, illogical, irrational linkages.

> How clean the sun when seen in its idea,
> Washed in the remotest cleanliness of a heaven
> That has expelled us and our images. (C.P. 381)

Here, absurdly, the sun is being washed. But the absurdity
of the image forces the reader to recall that the sun in
Stevens is a figure for phenomena, for the objects we perceive (§ 18). What is really being washed is the eye of the
perceiver: his myths, his images, are being washed away.

§ 4   The very limited, special, sometimes illogical relation
between a figure and what it represents, as in the jar, the hat,
and the sun, is all part of a larger double vision in Stevens,
a nominalist's view of language and its relation to reality,
a belief in the distinct separation of words and things.
Metaphor to Stevens is always evasion, all relations between
objects are created by the human mind, all formulations, the
relating of objects to ideas and feelings, are artificial,
fictional:

> There is nothing more inscribed nor thought nor felt
> And this must comfort the heart's core against
> Its false disasters—these fathers standing round,
> These mothers touching, speaking, being near,
> These lovers waiting in the soft dry grass. (C.P. 372)

Stevens here is free to exploit the shock value in naming
highly emotionally-charged figures "false disasters" because,
in fact, your father and mine are not at the center, but only
at the periphery of meaning in the figure. The fathers,

mothers and lovers represent all those personal longings, desires for permanence of the self and relation to the world, that the world is not constituted to satisfy. (It is wrong, Stevens is saying, to sap the spirit by impossible yearnings for the continuation of things as they once were, or for values that are more than expressions of shifting feelings.) I realize that it is hard to accept such an abstract reading at face value, but I intend the rest of this study to demonstrate that Stevens uses his figures in just such a limited way. The use of "fathers" to represent yearnings and desires not really for personal relations but for relation to reality in some absolute way is odd, but precise and accessible, a specialist's use. There is a fine tension in Stevens' figures between their common use and his own limited use. In Stevens' poems, the doctrinal progression is primary, the surface drama is an ironic or comic filigree. This will be seen again and again, as for example, in his figures of "women" (§ 22, 40, and 51), or of a corpse (§ 52), or of the elders who rape Susanna (§ 55). The worlds of perception and the worlds of imagination are distinct; what is true in the "mundo" is not in the real world; what the human ego really desires (permanence) is not what the poem can give.

It is perhaps evident now that I see the central problem Stevens dealt with in a lifetime of poems as that of analogic fallacy. He passionately believed in the power of the imagination to make at least a momentary order out of chaos by means of metaphor, but he saw clearly that such an irrational order can have only transitory value. The imagination is seen as both God and fake. Thus his vital figures, almost by reflex action, have two aspects—one of value, one of nothingness.

> To say the solar chariot is junk
> Is not a variation but an end.

> Yet to speak of the whole world as metaphor
> Is still to stick to the contents of the mind.
> And the desire to believe in a metaphor.
> It is to stick to the nicer knowledge of
> Belief, that what it believes in is not true.   (C.P. 332)

§ 5   That is quite distinctly a poet speaking, not a philosopher. Stevens never really pretended to be a philosopher. Indeed, the burden of his essay, "A Collect of Philosophy," is that philosophers are poets who have become entranced by the poetry of one idea or set of ideas. Stevens was finally an anti-rationalist who played with ideas, with the experience of thinking. In the same essay Stevens remarks, "The philosopher intends his integration to be fateful, the poet intends his to be effective." Effective, that is, as a flow of feelings, "a music of ideas." And so when one comes upon possible inconsistencies in the doctrinal aspects of Stevens' figures, it is simply a case of being involved with a new orchestration, a new attempt at projecting one of those

> . . . incalculable balances,
> At which a kind of Swiss perfection comes
>
> And a familiar music of the machine
> Sets up its Schwärmerei.   (C.P. 386)

And for those precious, transitory moments,

> Green is the path we take
> Between chimeras and garlanded the way,
> The down-descent into November's void.   (O.P. 67)

Characteristically, there is no attempt to evade mentioning in the same breath the ecstasy of the imaginative moment and the real 'machine," the November void. Stevens truly takes with one hand while giving with the other. This is the way he sees life—as a dynamic moving in and out of rare moments of equilibrium. And yet, of course, even these moments do not give the lasting sustenance to the spirit that T. S. Eliot would assert is given in a moment "at the still point of the turning world." Stevens' moments are ones of "golden illusion" (C.P. 107), and he can look only with irony and some wistfulness at Eliot's idea of a timeless moment:

He wanted his heart to stop beating and his mind to rest . . .

Just to know how it would feel, released from destruction,
To be a bronze man breathing under archaic lapis,

Without the oscillations of planetary pass-pass,
Breathing his bronzen breath at the azury centre of time.

(C.P. 425)

Stevens' moments are a kind of exalted hedonism, a sublime aestheticism, true, but this aestheticism is not presented with the lightness of the "tourist" that so many of Stevens' critics consider him.[2] It comes from a deeply felt need for answers within an ontological position, a position that discredits the

2. See Bibliography, under *Abel, Jarrell, Winters.* A given poem of Stevens can, of course, be attacked on other grounds. There are poems where Stevens engages in doctrinal polemic without the usual qualifying of view by an ironic figuration or filigree. Long parts of "An Ordinary Evening in New Haven" show this lack of tact, as do sections of many other poems. There are also poems, or sections of poems, where figures that have worked well in many contexts are so thrown together, by rote, as to give no clear images at all. This is what Randall Jarrell calls the mechanical operation of the "Method." See, for example, "Contrary Theses" (II), C.P. 270, where the argument is clear, but the figures are ineffective, do not augment one another.

rational process with its tendency to make one a "logical lunatic" committed to a set of ideas.[3]

§ 6   Stevens' great battle is not with the romantic or the positivist (the chimeras), but with himself, with the two sides of his own mind. "The poet represents the mind in the act of defending us against itself." (*Adagia,* O.P. 174) Stevens' poetry can be looked at most profitably, I think, as a continuous battle in his own mind over analogic fallacy, over imagination as value. There is discernible in Stevens, as many critics have pointed out, a slow drift toward a nominalist, subjectivist position. "When one is young everything is physical; when one is old everything is psychic" (Adagia, O.P. 167). The world of reality seemed at times but a phantasm of the imagination. But in any period of Stevens' writing, we are able to find poems or sections of poems that treat this incipient metaphysic with a conscious irony. It is indeed in a very late poem, "The World as Meditation," that one finds the quintessence of Stevens' double vision, the belief in the imagination and the awareness of its illusions, in the exquisite tension of:

> It was Ulysses and it was not.   (C.P. 521)

For the wretched human condition, the fears, the waiting and the wanting, the only recompense we have is locked in the mortal self. This is the ever-recurring answer in the poetry to the ever-recurring question,

> Where shall we find more than derisive words?
> When shall lush chorals spiral through our fire
> And daunt that old assassin, heart's desire?   (O.P. 66)

3.   R. P. Blackmur sees Stevens' best poems coming out of a "sensibility in desperation," "lyric cries, all the more moving because we feel in them a craving for a fuller being than they can ever reach." ("On Herbert Read and Wallace Stevens," see Bibliography).

The rest of this study will concern itself with detailed investigation of specific figures, figures in context, the structural frames of whole poems, and, incidentally, of the verbal ambiguities of which Stevens is such a master. Constant reference to the poetic texts will be made both to establish our reading, and, more importantly, to explicate or refine our understanding of passages and posture in many other poems. Finally, there will be an attempt to use the information gleaned from these anatomies to analyze, with some precision and sensitivity to the tensions and irresolutions present, several of Stevens' longer poems.

The scheme of classification that follows, as Figures of the Mind, of Disorder, of Order, and of Change, has admittedly some disadvantages. We are studying the consistent doubleness of Stevens' vision, and have asserted that a given figure, either within itself or through its contextual relations, disposes itself into two separate and opposing aspects. It is therefore reasonable (and correct) to assume that different aspects of the same figure will not lie together in a strict classification. However, I feel one can still handle the figures as entities, without an absurd anatomical dismemberment, by keeping in mind that a Stevens' figure has a doctrinal aspect and an ironic aspect. The former, that aspect of a figure that contributes to a coherent argument, indifferent to the wants and anguish of the human ego, can serve as the basis for classification of a figure. The irony, the welling up of the irrational human will in mockery or anguish, can be handled together with the doctrine, as it should be, since Stevens feels both concomitantly. There are disadvantages, too, in discussing the figures of the mind first, since these are generally the most abstract, the least vivid of Stevens' figures, coming mostly in the later poetry when ontology becomes more nakedly the subject of his poems. On the other hand, the discussion of the figures of the mind is perhaps the least painful way to approach Stevens' ideas, certainly less painful than through the kind of amateur philosophical discourse often used by critics. Then, too, the scheme parallels the operation of the whole imaginative process, as, the Perceiver, the Perceived, the Ordering, and the Dissolution.

Chapter Two

Figures of the Mind
(Reason and the Imagination)

Inescapable romance, inescapable choice
Of dreams, disillusion as the last illusion,
Reality as a thing seen by the mind,
Not that which is but that which is apprehended,
A mirror, a lake of reflections in a room. (C.P. 468)

§ 7 The passage is a characteristic one from the late Stevens, postulating a philosophic subjectivism in a poetry of statement interspersed with figures that now relate much less to one another than the figures in earlier poems. Rather, the figures of the last line, the mirror, the lake, the room, all have their own relation to aspects of the ontological position sketched in the lines above. "A mirror, a lake of reflections in a room," is not, to my mind, an effective conjugation, but it does help one to understand a whole cluster of recurring figures in the poems.

The mirror, rather than giving us any knowledge of what "is," merely reflects the jumble of apprehended objects as perceived by one's sensory apparatus:

The brown at the bottom of red
The orange far down in yellow,
Are falsifications from a sun

> In a mirror, without heat,
> In a constant secondariness. (C.P. 506)

Red is the color of reality unfalsified; yellow the sun's color cast on phenomena. "Brown" and "orange" are the falsifications of reality in the (warping) mirror of the mind. These falsifications are not the conscious distortions of the imagination, those "blues" and "greens," for "he looked in a glass of the earth and thought he lived in it." (C.P. 507) The desire to see in the mirror the world exactly as it is is implicit in the quotation, but explicit is the knowledge that the mind's mirror really reflects only the self in a "constant secondariness."

We are prepared now to approach these equivocal lines:

> The spirit comes from the body of the world,
> Or so Mr. Homburg thought: the body of a world
> Whose blunt laws make an affectation of mind,
> The mannerism of nature caught in a glass
> And there become a spirit's mannerism,
> A glass aswarm with things going as far as they can.
> (C.P. 519)

"Affectation" is consciously ambiguous, meaning, in one sense, "appearing to have some order," in another sense, "producing a parallel affectation or mannerism in the perceiving mind." We can know only nature's "mannerisms," and we mirror what we perceive in our own "spiritual" gestures. If what we call "spirit" is much dependent on the effects of nature on the mind, then the mind can, of course, not hope to transcend its (meaningless) mannerisms in a poem. But this is only Mr. Homburg's postulate, and he, of course, it limited in thought's mirrors, and hatted like everybody else. "Things going as far as they can," refers it seems, to this limitation of the mind's glass to the mannerisms of nature, "spirit" being really a product of "body."

The mind's boundaries are similarly projected as a house or a room where one is alone, or as walls which enclose one:

> He is what he hears and sees and if,
> Without pathos, he feels what he hears
> And sees, being nothing otherwise, he has not
> To go to the Louvre to behold himself.
> Granted each picture is a glass,
> That the walls are mirrors multiplied. (C.P. 194–5)

The Louvre, of course, has rooms containing spiritual gestures of man.

And the world simply cannot be grasped as a whole, the mystic garden known by the middling beast:

> These are his infernal walls,
> A space of stone, of inexplicable base
> And peaks outsoaring possible adjectives. (C.P. 185)

The imaginative act can, for a time, lift one from the mind's cell:

> Then from their poverty they rose,
> From dry catarrhs, and to guitars
> They flitted
> Through the palace walls. (C.P. 10)

But it must be noticed in this famous poem, "The Ordinary Women," that the inevitable return is to the limits of the mind in order to be, as it were, refreshed by reality.

> Then from their poverty they rose,
> From dry guitars, and to catarrhs

They flitted
Through the palace walls. (C.P. 12)

Neither side of the wall affords tranquility. Without the imagination we have "each man in his asylum maundering" (O.P. 68).

Even with the imagination operative, the "candle" burning, we have no more than the solitary man in a cold room, wrapped in a single shawl, within the "vital boundary, in the mind" (see C.P. 524). What the candle can do is to enlarge by means of projection the things in life that we, in our poverty, have left. "The hand between the candle and the wall grows large on the wall" (C.P. 245). The hand is in part a figure for the projection of the self driven by the will to make gestures on the wall. We must keep in mind this poignant image of the man alone in a room with the candle making gestures on the wall when we come across other, more noble presentations of the imagination's enlargements of reality.

There is not much left to say now about "lakes," and the "lake of reflections in a room." A lake surface is calmer than, say, the ocean, more like the mirror reflecting things. The ocean itself, unabstracted chaos, has too much motion to be contemplated by the mind: a lake is a better figure for the mind's dealings with reality. The mind abstracts slightly even before it begins the process of thought; a necessary falsification of reality is implicit in the imaginative act: "night's moonlight lake was neither water nor air." (O.P. 111)

§ 8   The mind cannot escape its walls, mirrors, lake surfaces, but its desire for "celestial ease" can be palliated by the imaginative "mundo," the world of ordered images as opposed to the world of objects. Will and Desire, the impulses which cause Stevens' double vision, are everywhere poignantly dramatized:

> Say next to holiness is the will thereto,
> And next to love is the desire for love,
> The desire for its celestial ease in the heart,
>
> Which nothing can frustrate, that most secure,
> Unlike love in possession of that which was
> To be possessed and is. But this cannot
>
> Possess. It is desire, set deep in the eye,
> Behind all actual seeing, in the actual scene,
> In the street, in a room, on a carpet or a wall,
>
> Always in emptiness that would be filled. (C.P. 467)

§ 9   Will and desire are the "arms" with which the "soldier" fights his continual "war" against emptiness and chaos or against false abstraction and outworn fictions: "the brightness of arms, the will opposed to cold" (C.P. 273). One association of a figure wars upon another, the mind wars with itself. Stevens sees the conflicting elements in the mind as the necessary condition of man's life:

> The mind is the great poem of winter, the man,
> Who, to find what will suffice,
> Destroys romantic tenements
> Of rose and ice
>
> It has to content the reason concerning war,
> It has to persuade that war is part of itself,
> A manner of thinking, a mode
> Of destroying, as the mind destroys. (C.P. 238-9)[1]

1. For "Winter," see § 16.

The "soldier" seeks the moments of equilibrium (see § 5) between chaos and a false order, the

> . . . point between the two,

> The organic consolation, the complete
> Society of the spirit when it is
> Alone, the half-arc hanging in mid-air
> Composed, appropriate to the incomplete,
> Supported by a half-arc in mid-earth. (C.P. 309)[2]

From these 'moments" of peace come the imaginative fictions which sustain the world:

> Integration for integration, the great arms
> Of the armies, the solid men, make big the fable. (C.P. 301)

The "soldiers of time" never cease to suffer and finally succumb in the mind's war, but beauty comes from the suffering and death: "how red the rose that is the soldier's wound" (C.P. 318). These integrations are not final absolutes. The soldier must go on fighting old integrations and creating new ones, the business of "Gigantomachia" ("Giants' war"):

> Millions of major men against their like
> Make more than thunder's rural rumbling. They make
> The giants that each one of them becomes
> In a calculated chaos. (C.P. 307)[3]

§ 10   There is something very pathetic about what Stevens' twentieth-century soldier is fighting for. The plight calls to mind Shelley's "tis we who lost in stormy visions,

---

2. For "half-arc" and its relation to a full "circle," see § 12.
3. For "giant," "Major Man," and a fuller analysis of this passage, see § 42.

keep with phantoms an unprofitable strife." And Stevens is of two minds about the war. An awareness of the futility in what the poet is doing is present as an undertone in two related figures that occur often in Stevens' poetry, "ghosts" and "shadows."

For Stevens, there is no evidence for an immortal soul and so, in the best light, man's "ghost" is equated with the imaginative faculty within him, the faculty impelled by will and desire to seek out 'ghostlier demarcations, keener sounds" (C.P. 130) in the phenomenological world. In the worst light, of course, ghosts are hallucinations of the ignorant. Rationalists create ghostly sequences which are best discarded:

> This structure of ideas, these ghostly sequences
> Of the mind, result only in disaster. . . .
>
> It is more difficult to evade
> That habit of wishing and to accept the structure
> Of things as the structure of ideas. (C.P. 326–7)

Our "ghosts" have a predilection for imagining their dominance of "things." Even the rabbit sees his ghost as King of the Ghosts: "you become a self that fills the four corners of night" (C.P. 209). But the imagination must always give up these pretensions and return to the "structure of things," as read by the "large red man": [4]

> There were ghosts that returned to earth to hear his phrases,
> As he sat there reading, aloud, the great blue tabulae.
>
> (C.P. 423)

4. The red man is, like the red bird, a figure for reality, but reality a bit "turned." He is "large," a projection (see "giant," § 42) of the imagination's "blue." For "blue," see below, footnote no. 7. The ambiguous ghost that haunts "The Idea Of Order at Key West" is discussed by Arthur Mizener in the *Kenyon Review*, 1951, pp. 212–15.

Shadows, like ghosts, are cast by the candle of the imagination, fed by desire. Any "shadow" that once pleased, say the waltz, will sooner or later cease to please:

> There comes a time when the waltz
> Is no longer a mode of desire, a mode
> Of revealing desire and is empty of shadows. (C.P. 121)

But shadows are as necessary to life as hats. In the dialogue that informs the "Man with the Blue Guitar," it is the "angelic ones," those desiring celestial permanence, who lament,

> There are no shadows in our sun,
> Day is desire and night is sleep.
> There are no shadows anywhere.
> The earth, for us, is flat and bare.
> There are no shadows. (C.P. 167)

The sun of blank (or "blunt") reality shines too brightly.[5] The imagination is seen as "the noble figure, the essential shadow" (C.P. 223). There is one side of the mind that will project the imagination's shadows so as to inform the universe with Major Man, its fictive god:

> Now, I . . . speak of this shadow as
> A human thing. It is an eminence,
> But of nothing, trash of sleep that will disappear
> With the special things of night. (C.P. 300)

There is another side of the mind, that was ever old and

5. Again, an image from Shelley comes to mind: "On the withering flower the killing sun smiles brightly" ("Adonais," XXXII). Stevens seems to have Shelley's imagery well in hand, as if he considered him the archetypal romantic poet. George Santayana, Stevens' favorite philosopher, treats Shelley as such, in a masterful and affectionate essay on him.

bitter, that sees the shadows, in restrospect, as only phantoms:[6]

> . . . The houses still stand,
> Though they are rigid in rigid emptiness.

> Even our shadows, their shadows, no longer remain.
> The lives these lived in the mind are at an end.
> They never were. . . . (C.P. 525)

§ 11   In the poem, "The Common Life," Stevens com-
plains of "the shadows that are absent from Euclid," and
describes the morbid light that is cast on the page. This
morbid light, I take it, is the best refraction of the sun that
the reason can make. Reason in Stevens' figuration is seen
in terms of straight lines, sharp angles, squares, and truncated
geometrical figures.

> Day after day, throughout the winter,
> We hardened ourselves to live by bluest reason
> In a world of wind and frost,

> And by will, unshaken and florid
> In mornings of angular ice,
> That passed beyond us through the narrow sky. (C.P. 124)[7]

6. W. R. Keast in an essay on "Thirteen Ways of Looking at a
    Blackbird," in the *Chicago Review,* Vol. 8, No. 1, makes a nice
    distinction between the aesthetically pleasing shadow of the
    blackbird in stanza VI, and the shadow of mortality cast by
    the poet's "equipage" in stanza XI.
7. Blue here is not the color of the imagination as it is usually said
    to be without qualification. Stevens is clear about the two-
    headedness of this figure:

    > The sky will be much friendlier then than now,
    > A part of labor and a part of pain,
    > And next in glory to enduring love,
    > Not this dividing and indifferent blue. (C.P. 68)

What has passed beyond is time, time when the mind could have lived in an imaginative "mundo." Reality can be approached by reason, but the result is an inhuman geometric cosmos that is neither the romantic's cradle nor any poet's "mundo":

> The lines are straight and swift between the stars.
> The night is not the cradle that they cry,
> The criers, undulating the deep-oceaned phrase.
> The lines are much too dark and much too sharp.
>
> The mind herein attains simplicity.
> There is no moon, on single, silvered leaf.   (C.P. 71)[8]

§ 12   A tolerable world can be created for oneself only by the twisting of the straight lines of reason into an imaginative deviation from reality:

> It was when the trees were leafless first in November
> And their blackness became apparent, that one first
> Knew the eccentric to be the base of design.   (C.P. 151)

One of the "Adagia" reads: "The absolute object slightly turned is a metaphor of the object," since it is not the real thing any more, but an "evasion" of reality, a "revealing aberration":

> These pods are part of the growth of life within life:
> Part of the unpredictable sproutings . . .
>
> That could come in a slight lurching of the scene,
> A swerving, a tilting, a little lengthening.   (O.P. 92)

The words Stevens uses to describe the process of the imaginative molding of reality shows his ambivalent attitude

8. The "moon" casts the light of the imagination, as contrasted to reality's "sunlight." Its color is silver, not "yellow."

toward the process: wrinklings, dodgings, writhings, crisp-
ing, bending, perverting, tilting, lurching, twistings, swerv-
ings, quirks, distortions, contortions, malformations, oblique,
astray, askew and awry. But also it is curling, curving,
curvetting, swaying, winding, wreathing, turning, the ellipse
and the arc. Rosenbloom (C.P. 79) was "wry" and "wizened"
because he had turned from reality, but in a wholly supernatural way. The revolutionists (C.P. 102) who stop for
orangeade, standing in the sun, cannot go on paying obeis-
ance to the real, to the "capitan geloso," since "there is no
pith in music except in something false." They must have
refreshment, and, in our time, this can only come from a
wholly conscious, and therefore comic, warping of the real:

> Wear a helmet without reason,
> Tufted, tilted, twirled, and twisted.
>
> Hang a feather by your eye,
> Nod and look a little sly.
> This must be the vent of pity,
> Deeper than a truer ditty
> Of the real that wrenches,
> Of the quick that's wry. (C.P. 103)

"Wrenches' 'and "wry" here are painfully ambiguous. The
imagination twists reality, but also reality twists the human
heart and forces one into absurd posturings in order to
endure it. An imaginative artifice creates a new elliptical
reality which does not wrench:

> Here the total artifice reveals itself
>
> As the total reality. Therefore it is
> One says even of the odor of this fruit,
> That steeps the room, quickly, then not at all,

> It is more than the odor of this core of earth
> And water. It is that which is distilled
> In the prolific ellipses that we know
>
> In the planes that tilt hard revelations on
> The eye, a geometric glitter, tiltings
> As of sections collecting toward the greenest cone.
>
> "Someone Puts a Pineapple Together," III (N.A. 87)

But always the odor comes and goes. The final figure in the quotation is one from solid geometry, the "planes," the "ellipses," the "sections" (metaphors) "tilt" the hard revelations of perception, and collect toward a cone whose apex is at the center of a sphere, the pineapple, "primitive orb."[9]

§ 13 The usual figure to sum up Stevens' attitude towards all these various "curvings" of reality is the circle. And like all of Stevens' figures when they are fully explored, this obvious culminating of all curves and arcs is something to be avoided:

> He called hydrangeas purple. [they are white] And they
>   were.
> Not fixed and deadly (like a curving line
>   that merely makes a ring).
> It was a purple changeable to see (O.P. 23–4)

Once the warping is made the warped form is fixed, and so no longer delights. To live too long within an imaginative mundo is to be locked in a closed circle that is just as tedious as the rational process (that always returns us to our poverty of spirit).[10] All the mind's operations are circular, except,

---

9. The pineapple is a natural, not geometric form, three dimensional, not two (like reason's circle), a good figure for the world of reality grasped as a whole by the imagination. (See Chap. 11, Pt. 2, Sec. 5).
10. Ralph Mills, Jr., in an essay, "Wallace Stevens: the Image of the Rock" in *Accent,* XVIII, No. 2, and also, W. R. Keast, *ibid.,*

perhaps, in the irrational flash of the imagination which colors our world and allows us to avoid the blankness of the centre :

> In the punctual centre of all circles white
> Stands truly. (C.P. 366)

§ 14   White and black are the polarities of the mind's spectrum of mood, and both are pernicious. The "black sublime" is death (O.P. 55), and every functioning of this color revolves around death. White brings us to the void by the opposite direction, by the obliteration of all color in life through the operations of the intellect or by the fading away of an imaginative world, as in :

> A blue pigeon it is, that circles the blue sky,
> On sidelong wing, around and round and round.
> A white pigeon it is, that flutters to the ground,
> Grown tired of flight. (C.P. 17)

or :

> A blue scene washing white in the rain, (C.P. 306)

The weeping burgher (C.P. 61) distorts reality to create fictions which, alas, grow old soon in their "excess" :

> And I, then, tortured for old speech,
> A white of wildly woven rings;
> I, weeping in a calcined heart,
> My hands such sharp, imagined things. (C.P. 61)[11]

Reality in another poem is figured by a parakeet whose green feathers are forms that please our eye, but whose

discuss "circles" from perspectives different from the above, but which do not contradict anything said.
11. For "hands," see § 29.

"lids are white because his eyes are blind" (C.P. 82).[12] The "white elders" who ravish Susanna are figures for reality's victory over the green "garden" of her creation.[13] An old fiction becomes a "white abstraction" merely (C.P. 276). Whiteness is the "ultimate intellect" (C.P. 433), when all motion ceases, and, therefore, all life, color and mood does too. We long for rest, but rest is either death or sleep; "in the punctual center of all circles white stands truly." (C.P. 366).

The other color figures in Stevens' spectrum were among the first figures to be treated by Stevens' critics, and I have very little to add except to remind the reader of the ambiguity we have seen in the color "blue," and to urge him to be wary of relating a given color to one sort of emotion only. One must keep Stevens' double way of seeing things in mind at every point in reading his poems. Why, for example, does he say, "Pink and white carnations—one desires so much more than that?" (C.P. 193) We know how "white" is loaded, what then of "pink"? The first association is one of the mawkishness, the prettiness of pink, too bland for poems of strength in an honest facing-up to reality. But we are also to remember that pink is a mixture (or fading) of red with white. Red being the color of unabstracted reality in all its harshness, we see that the statement, in fact, says that we desire so much more than reality can offer us. Pink is a stronger color than we want, part of a cold astringent scene:

> . . . The day itself
> Is simplified: a bowl of white,
> Cold, a cold porcelain, low and round,
> With nothing more than the carnations there. (C.P. 193)

12. For "feathers," see § 19, 39.
13. See Chapter 7 for a full analysis of "Peter Quince."

Brown is close to black and so is close to death. Gold is precious, but it is also the color of the sun's ray. Purple is a deeper blue than the sky affords, an augmented delight and a greater distortion. Bronze is a sun-color and a cold permanent metal. Green is the color of life, but also the color of reality without spirit.

§ 15   The geography of the mind and its seasons, as Stevens sees them, have also been much studied by Stevens' critics, and the attempt here will be only to see these clusters of figures in terms of our approach to Stevens.

Bordeaux is in the East, from Crispin's point of view. He follows the sun from Europe across the Atlantic to the West, America. (He goes first to South America, the Yucatan, and then to the North, Carolina.) The Palace of Hoon is in the East. All of Europe and the Orient is the East to Stevens. The East, in other words, implies the cultures of the past, and Crispin, modern man, lives in their backwash, as

> The ribboned stick, the bellowing breeches, cloak
> Of China, cap of Spain. (C.P. 28)

These cultures no longer suffice, the trappings of the old orders remain, but they no longer embody a reality. Stevens has mixed feelings about their passing.[14] Crispin does not make his voyage west for pleasure, as a tourist. He makes it because he has to, because of the "westwardness of everything," seemingly culture to anarchy, and, most certainly, day to night, life to death:

> Light, too, encrusts us, making visible
> The motions of the mind and giving form
> To moodiest nothings, as, desire for day

14. For a full analysis of "The Comedian as the Letter C" see
    Chapter 9.

> Accomplished in the immensely flashing East,
> Desire for rest, in that descending sea
> Of dark, which in its very darkening
> Is rest and silence spreading into sleep. (C.P. 137)

"Encrusts' 'is ambiguous, meaning, first, a binding of us to "moodiest nothings," but then also a valuable "giving form to," as in a poem of the imagination:

> The whole habit of the mind is changed by them
> These Gaeled and fitful-fangled darknesses
> Made suddenly luminous, themselves a change,
> An east in their compelling westwardness. (C.P. 455)

East and West then represent light and darkness, the tragic chiaroscuro.

North and South are chromatic, and appear to mean such a welter of things to Stevens in different contexts that it is difficult to speak here with any precision. Perhaps the basic dichotomy between North and South in Stevens' mind is that in the North one is in twentieth-century society, while in the South one is more alone with chaotic, exotic reality.[15] But both North and South are fusions of the real with the imaginative, and both necessarily have their tragic aspects. Crispin cannot stay in the Yucatan for the thunderstorms, and yet the voyager in "Farewell to Florida" has no illusions about what he will find in the North:

> The leaves in which the wind kept up its sound
> From my North of cold whistled in a sepulchral South,
>
> (C.P 117)

15. The first stanza of "Academic Discourse in Havana," contrasting the "wilderness" and the "metropoles," gives, in figurative language, a good sense of the North-South distinction.

My North is leafless and lies in a wintry slime
Both of men and clouds, a slime of men in crowds.

(C.P. 118)

One's mind is not going to be at rest in either its northern or
southern aspects, and the tired spirit, even in the early
Stevens, can shrink from them both:

Let us fix portals, east and west,
Abhorring green-blue north and blue-green south. (O.P. 17)

Geographical reference is everywhere in Harmonium, but
a little thought on the simpler facts of the locale render these
figures accessible enough. The sky is very blue in Oklahoma;
Key West and Cuba are both islands in the ocean; the Indies
are wild and the Indians on them primitive, etc., etc.

§ 16   The figures of the seasons of the mind present few
problems to Stevens' critics. There is of course the prevailing
irony of the eternal cycles of the "generations of the imagination" (C.P. 434) contrasted with the mortal fate of the poet
and his cycles of creation. This same irony appears also in
the heavily ambiguous aspects of Night, as a good time for
the imagination, and a bad time for personal fears of mortality. Winter, like Night, serves as the tragic background upon
which light and life play. Winter is when the mind destroys
imaginative worlds created in summer. The winter mind, as
Stevens sees it, is not a state brought on by the absolute perception of real objects. This is impossible. We all see things
through the veils of our senses. He asserts in "The Plain
Sense of Things," "The absence of the imagination had
itself to be imagined" (C.P. 502). Winter, therefore, is just
another metaphor, the fabric of another dream:

Now it is September and the web is woven.
The web is woven and you have to wear it.

> The winter is made and you have to bear it,
> The winter web, the winter woven, wind and wind
> It is the mind that is woven. (C.P. 208)

The mind's landscape, without the intensest flame of the imagination, is always wintry and destructive:

> The mind is the great poem of winter, the man,
> Who, to find what will suffice,
> Destroys romantic tenements[16]
> Of rose and ice
>
> In the land of war. (C.P. 238–9)

§ 17 The imagination's workings, its seasons, its colorings, its wars, are hardly voluntary. In that late figure of the mind, the child asleep in its own life, we have the culmination of all the confusion and beauty that has come from a lifetime of facing the "dumbfoundering abyss between us and the object." (C.P. 437) No more haunting projection of subjectiveness could perhaps be found than that of an ignorant, innocent child in a world of dreams. The child looks straight at the object with wonder, asking "Mother, what is that?" The "drowsy, infant" old man still has only questions to ask, but they are even more futile, subjective questions: "Mother, my mother, who are you?" (C.P. 462)

The mind, as child, therefore, being so isolated, creates out of its own need the "forms of dark desire" (C.P. 432) for sleep, peace, and relation with the exterior world.[17] All

16. "Tenement" is precise, meaning both "a thing held," and an old outworn edifice.
17. "The Owl in the Sarcophogus" (C.P. 431–6). The owl seems to figure the fears of personal death that make life a near-death for many people. The owl appears, in an enigmatic way, on C.P. 243, 244 and 245. The imaginative man attempts to create a mythos from within himself to combat these fears (see further § 19).

three of the figures for these desires, "monsters of elegy" in a "mythology of modern death," exhibit in the poem the *ultimate* futility of figures.

> . . . Sleep realized
> Was the whiteness that is the ultimate intellect, (C.P. 433)

But the mind cannot help bringing forth children of desire, images of itself at war with itself, any more than the child can, in its cycle of life, deny his instinct for creation:

> The children of a desire that is the will,
> Even of death, the beings of the mind
> In the light-bound space of the mind, the floreate
>   flare. . . .
>
> It is a child that sings itself to sleep,
> The mind, among the creatures that it makes,
> The people, those by which it lives and dies. (C.P. 436)

Chapter Three

Figures of Disorder
(Reality, Chaos, Parts of a World)

Life is a bitter aspic. We are not
at the centre of a diamond. (C.P. 322)

§ 18   An aspic is a gelatine mass with little pieces of meat,
egg, or fish embedded here and there. The aspic, Stevens
asserts in "Esthetique du Mal" X, is analogous to what one
can make out of the world without the Imagination. We
recognize particulars, parts, in the mass but we can recognize
no coherent order. The "sun" is an "eye only" (C.P. 252);
there is no mind apparent in phenomena. The sun's "classic"
arrangement is one of no perceivable arrangement. It was
the old philosophy that saw the universe as a diamond with
every object and being in it at its appointed position, with
everything relating to man as the centre, a universe brilliant
with values, cut hard and clear for eternity by the diamond
master, God the creator. The diamond order was a beautiful
order, but a false one. Within it, one saw death-in-war as
noble, leading to some supernatural end; one saw the wind
and weather as the helpers of man guided on his course by
angels; one saw the church as holding a truth beyond the
chaotic facts of sense perception; one saw nature as existing
for man's use. The twentieth-century poet has not the riches
of the old philosophy. In his poverty, he has hardly enough

to endure, and his diet must of necessity consist of the aspic. And since there is no other real food, he comes with time to prefer it to the confects of an outworn philosophy, confects which finally are bitter in the extreme in their untruth.' The bitterness of the truth, however, is sweet in the expressing of it; these "exacerbations" become "epicure" in their ordering, their arrangement in the poetic imagination. But Stevens does not falsify the essence of the process when he calls it:

Hunger feeding on its own hungriness.   (C.P. 323)

Crispin, at home in his village, had been used to berries, apricots, and salad beds, but once out to sea, and hungry, it is different: "one eats one's paté, even of salt, quotha." The salty paté is a food quite like the aspic, and probably embodies, in addition, an audacious pun on paté—one eats one's head, quotha. There is nothing outside of the mind in the external world to feed on as value; one feeds on one's own hungriness, on one's desire for order, on oneself.

Again, the world, when the imagination is ineffective, is a "dry loaf" (another edible) to the hunger for order ("Dry Loaf," C.P. 199). Life in the thirties was a desperate grasping for the loaf only. And yet, from within man, even in his poverty, more sustenance could come, images from out of the imagination, to

. . . the dry men blown
Brown as the bread, thinking of birds

1. These lines about the aspic and the diamond are justly famous, and exert a magical power over the reader so that he does not notice that the figures are part of a mixed metaphor. The aspic is a food, the diamond is not. Also, life could be a bitter aspic, and yet man could still be at the centre of the diamond. The two statements are not really related.

Flying from burning countries and brown sand shores.

(C.P. 199–200)[2]

This is not to say that the imaginative order, figured as the bird in flight, has any permanence, that reality will ever be understood or finally ordered.

> The world, a turnip once so readily plucked,
> Sacked up and carried overseas, daubed out
> Of its ancient purple, pruned to the fertile main,
> And sown again by the stiffest realist,
> Came reproduced in purple, family font,
> The same insoluble lump. The fatalist
> Stepped in and dropped the chuckling down his craw,
> Without grace or grumble.   (C.P. 45)

Crispin once thought he knew all about reality, had "daubed" and "pruned" the crude turnip, but he comes to see that solving one problem only gives birth to many more. The imagination, only, can handle this "family font" of insoluble problems by accepting the lumpy turnip as one's food, and imagining it good.

Stevens' use of the aspic, turnip, loaf and paté figures to represent his complex view of reality is not wholly characteristic of all his figures dealing with reality and chaos. Stevens often simply selects a particular from the external world and uses it in an emblematic way to represent that world. The context, then, generates the complexity, usually through a direct statement of the poet's mood in conflict with the emblem's implications about the external world (see for example "The Man on the Dump," C.P. 201). There is a plethora of animals and plants, especially flowers ("azaleas,

2. For "birds in flight" as a figure for reality ordered, in control, see § 39.

and so on"), and natural landscapes that are not at all ambiguous in intent and which, as a result, are usually so accessible as not to warrant discussion here. The lion, the elephant, the bear, and the worm, or, say, the iris, hepatica and the lilac have all, to be sure, their own particular ambience, and are not arbitrarily placed in Stevens' poems, but, like the women in "The Common Life," they "have only one side." Having said this to explain the exclusion of many prevalent figures of Stevens, we can consider now those figures of reality which do have something like a double signification.

§ 19   We have already mentioned the parakeet with the coppery keen claws (see § 14) as a figure for reality, blind, indifferent, but with a blazing tail and natural dazzle—the true *materia poetica*:

> He munches a dry shell while he exerts
> His will, yet never ceases, perfect cock
> To flare, in the sun-pallor of his rock.   (C.P. 82)[3]

This is a dry bird of sun and rock and yet we have seen the "dry men" find sustenance in the dreams of flying birds (C.P. 200). There is no discrepancy. Birds are real objects of a red, real world, but the flights of birds, their arcs, feathers, tails, their cries and songs, are all aspects of birds that the imagination fastens on as analogs of complex ideas of order. These aspects will be discussed later as figures of order, and it will be there that the complexity of the bird figures in Stevens can be more fully demonstrated.

One bird is, however, in Stevens, a simple figure for reality—the clawing cock. The cock's crow awakens the

3.   For "rock," see § 25.

hearer from his sleep of dreams back to reality. (The Shelleyan lark is the figure for those dreams)[4]:

> . . . . There is no place,
> Here, for the lark fixed in the mind,
> In the museum of the sky. The cock
> Will claw sleep. (C.P. 182)

The cock existed before man came to assert his centrality in a diamond design of the world: "the best cock of red feather . . . crew before the clocks" (C.P. 89). Stevens says that we must make our own diamonds out of the real, out of pain. There are those people who, while doubting the truth of cosmic design still, in their fears, also distrust the imagination that can make diamonds out of the painful aspic truth,

> The people that turned off and came
> To avoid the bright, discursive wings,
> To avoid the hap-hallow hallow-ho
> Of central things,
>
> Nor in their empty hearts to feel
> The blood-red redness of the sun,
> To shrink to an insensible,
> Small oblivion,
>
> Beyond the keenest diamond day
> Of people sensible to pain,
> When cocks wake, clawing at their beds
> to be again,
>
> And who, for that, turn toward the cocks
> And toward the start of day

4.   Nightingales and swans also figure outworn romantic attitudes. (The peacock is something else again and will be discussed later).

. . . he that suffers most desires
The red bird most and the strongest sky—
Not the people in the air that hear
The little owl fly. (C.P. 243–4)[5]

§ 20   But the desire for the "red bird" is a desire fraught
with hedges. The complete desire is not to run straight into
the jaws of reality, the fire-cat (C.P. 3), but to "swerve" away
from him, as the bucks do, in "circular" lines, till finally, the
firecat, temporarily spent, closes his bright eyes and sleeps.
For in reality there is ferocity, as in man there are two selves
and one is animal. The animal in us is part of reality, enjoys
the sensual, and is figured as the "subman" in "Owl's
Clover," (O.P. 66–8).

He was born within us as a second self,
A self of parents who have never died,
Whose lives return, simply, upon our lips,
Their words and ours, in what we see, their hues
Without a season. (O.P. 67)[6]

The other self, the anima, fears for its life near the firecat,
rejects its mortal, subman self (the animal), and wishes to
think about, make fictions of, the real peaches, rather than
merely look at and taste them (see C.P. 224). But the
"subman" asserts himself:

5. For "owl" see § 17n.
6. The various references to "niggers," "kinky clan," "black men,"
    etc., seem to connote this subman self: primitive, full of wonder,
    awe, and confused mysticism, of prayer and chants, living in the
    South and close to the earth. See C.P. 126, 145, 148, 150, 195,
    265, 415 and O.P. 9, 20, 56, 58, 59, 90 for the significant
    references. The "nigger" self is, of course, not the whole man. In
    stanza 7 of "Sunday Morning" (C.P. 70) we have the boistrous
    ring of men devoted to the "sun." Men that perish, men of dew,
    cannot feel for very long the orgiastic delight Stevens imbues
    them with. They will sing only on a "summer morn." The

> Who speaks? But it must be that I,
> That animal, . . . that exile, for whom
> The bells of the chapel pullulate sounds at
> Heart. The peaches are large and round,
> Ah! and red.
>
> The windows are open. The sunlight fills
> The curtains. Even the drifting of the curtains,
> Slight as it is, disturbs me. I did not know
> That such ferocities could tear
> One self from another, as these peaches do.   (C.P. 224)[7]

One self (the animal) enjoys being a "botanist," looking closely at the things of the earth; the other self (the anima) finds it cold on the "Alp," viewing a 'panorama of despair" (C.P. 135).

§ 21   The poet attempts to make words of the panorama, to be "conversant" with reality, but reality is a "monster":

> It is not a voice that is under the eaves.
> It is not speech, the sound we hear
> In this conversation, but the sound
> Of things and their motion: the other man,
> A turquoise monster moving round.   (C.P. 359–360)[8]

The man with the blue guitar hopes:

> That I may reduce the monster to
> Myself, and then may be myself
> In face of the monster, be more than part
> Of it, more than the monstrous player of
> One of its monstrous lutes.   (C.P. 175)

poignant irony in the stanza and in the last two lines particularly is almost lost, so persuasive is the joy of the summer chant.
7. For 'curtains" see § 43.
8. For "turquoise" see "purple" § 14.

But the imaginative dominance of things is not the truth. The truth of the world is an atomism which, for the human spirit in its need, can hardly suffice:

> . . . all these things together,
> Parts, and more things, parts. He never supposed divine
> Things might not look divine, nor that if nothing
> Was divine then all things were, the world itself,
> And that if nothing was the truth, then all
> Things were the truth, the world itself was the truth.
>
> (C.P. 242)

And finally, rather than ever attaining a constant imaginative dominance over reality, the continual struggle with the monster pushes one to a subjective acedia about struggling to know it at all:

> And though one says that one is part of everything,
> There is a conflict, there is a resistance involved;
> And being part is an exertion that declines. (O.P. 96)

§ 22 Reality, when it is out of control, is figured by Stevens as a monster. When in equilibrium, he sees reality as, say, the rude, the vulgar Indian, or the large red man reading. When Stevens' imagination is in control of reality, he sees reality as a woman who fascinates him, who dreams of "marriage" (abstraction into an ordered fictive "mundo"), but who is changeable of mood. Consider the "ordinary women" (C.P. 10), as objects unassimilated by the imagination and so in "poverty" and "monotony." The imagination removes them from their Harem-Prison by means of "heavenly script" (the poem), the "canting [slanting] curliques" that make explicit in "puissant speech" the beauty of real things slightly wrought or "pointed." The marriage, the assimilation of "things" into a poem is wrought easily (nonchalant) by moonlight. But the marriage, being unreal, cannot last, and a return to unassimilated reality (catarrhs) is then desired. Similarly, the "donna, donna dark," otherwise Florida, "venereal soil," is reality figured as a woman that will not be denied, returning always after an imaginative order (the music of the guitar) has been made:

> Swiftly in the nights,
> In the porches of Key West,
> Behind the bougainvilleas,
> After the guitar is asleep,
>
> Lasciviously as the wind,
> You come tormenting,
> Insatiable. (C.P. 47–8)

§ 23   Reality, the ocean of things perceived, the "sea of ex" (C.P. 175), always gets out of control simply through its incomprehensible vastness. We attempt an ordering and guard it jealously against chaos:

> These are within what we permit, in-bar
> Exquisite in poverty against the suns
> of ex-bar. (C.P. 317)

The ordering is the poem, but implicit in the poem which "resists the intelligence almost successfully" (C.P. 350) are overtones of the uncontrollability of reality, figured in the "storm":

> Things floating like the first hundred flakes of snow
> Out of a storm we must endure all night
> Out of a storm of secondary things. (C.P. 351)

Professor Eucalyptus in "An Ordinary Evening in New Haven" will not look beyond objects, the chaotic rain of things:

> He sits in his room, beside
> The window, close to the ramshackle spout in which
> The rain falls with a ramshackle sound. (C.P. 475)

He knows the ordering of this awful chaos comes only from within, from the creation of a fictive landscape:

> He preserves himself against the repugnant rain
> By an instinct for a rainless land, the self
> Of his self, come at upon wide delvings of wings.

Yet Stevens, with his characteristic ambivalent feeling toward unabstracted reality, cannot live in a "rainless land" for long, so that in another poem "the cataracts as facts fall like rejuvenating rain." (C.P. 263)

The figure of rain takes on a less emblematic, more symbolic character in a poem, "Human Arrangement," which is one of the fine expressions of what I feel is the essential Stevens: a poet perfectly aware of the human situation in its vacuous moments, and of the pathos of his answer for that vacuity. The rain of things upon the mind is matched by a chaotic rain of thought, mixed with desire. Imaginative shiftings of unreal forms are impelled by a will to repose, figured in the chair:

> Place-bound and time-bound in evening rain
> And bound by a sound which does not change,
>
> Except that it begins and ends,
> Begins again and ends again—
>
> Rain without change within or from
> Without. In this place and in this time
>
> And in this sound, which do not change,
> In which the rain is all one thing,

> In the sky, an imagined, wooden chair
> Is the clear-point of an edifice,
>
> Forced up from nothing, evening's chair,
> Blue-strutted curule, true—unreal,
>
> The centre of transformations that
> Transform for transformation's self,
>
> In a glitter that is a life, a gold
> That is a being, a will, a fate. (C.P. 363)

§ 24   The sound that does not change is the desolate fundamental tone of the universe. It is the romantic who in the sound of wind and leaves will find his own misery, for "here in the west indifferent crickets chant through our indifferent crises" (C.P. 321). The mind attuned to winter sound, the mind of the snowman, will not engage in futile pathetic fallacy or think his misery has any meaning, except to himself, in the larger landscape:

> The leaves cry. It is not a cry of divine attention,
> Nor the smoke-drift of puffed-out heroes, nor human cry.
> It is the cry of leaves that do not transcend themselves,
>
> In the absence of fantasia. (O.P. 96–7)

However, the poet, though he must respond to this fundamental tone, which has the prerogative of being the sound of the real, modulates it to a modest affirmation of the imagination's endurance beneath the storms of rain or snow.

> He seeks an image certain as meaning is
>
> To sound, sound's substance and executant,
> The particular tingle in a proclamation

That makes it say the little thing it says,

Below the prerogative jumble. (N.A. 84)

The first couple of lines bristle with ambiguities. The desire of the poet is not modest, the achievement is. He seeks an image; he will not find one. Meaning is not "certain" to sound. The image can be meaning's "executant" only in approximating, in a complex way, a complex set of feelings in the poet.

§ 25   The image that Stevens found that served him best, the figure that best enclosed in itself all of his attitudes toward reality, was the image of the rock.

> The world [was a] . . .
> Rock, of valedictory echoings
>
> To which his imagination returned
> From which it sped. (C.P. 179)
>
> Lord of the land and lord
> Of the men that live in the land. (C.P. 176)

As we have seen, Stevens admits the limits of perception. Reality to the eye is

> A space of stone, of inexplicable base
> And peaks outsoaring possible adjectives. (C.P. 185)

And "the rock cannot be broken." (C.P. 375) All we know, and can hope to know, is the material world of which we are a part:

> It is true that you live on the rock,
> And in it. It is wholly you. (O. P. 88)

Poetry itself, Stevens says in his introduction to *The Necessary Angel,* is "the movement of a self in the rock."

The conception of reality in terms of this image of the rock, as the "grey particular of man's life," seems to me to be perfectly accessible;[9] what is left to be examined are its ramifications.

In the face of the rock and only the rock, it is clearly up to man as poet, with his imagination, his "interior paramour," to make of life what he can:

> There was neither voice nor crested image,
> No chorister, nor priest. There was
> Only the great height of the rock
> And the two of them standing still to rest.   (C.P. 126)[10]

> The poem makes meanings of the rock,
> Of such mixed motion and such imagery
> That its barrenness becomes a thousand things
> And so exists no more.   (C.P. 527)

To obliterate the image of reality from the mind is finally the only "cure." The imaginative act abstracts from the rock until the rock becomes

> The weight we lift with the finger of a dream,
> The heaviness we lighten by light will,
> By the hand of desire.   (C.P. 476)

Mrs. Alfred Uruguay climbs the mountain, the real, on her

9. At any rate, since Ralph J. Mills, Jr.'s fine essay, "The Image of the Rock," in *Accent,* Spring, 1958. He speaks of Stevens' vision of "nothingness" and says, "The *barren* rock itself is the substance of this negation, though human assertions come to bear the "green leaves" upon it. It stands alone . . . an inhuman universe, and it remains meaningless, a raw fact, without the invasion of the mind and senses." (p. 86)
10. Voices, crested choristers, and priests, all chanters of mythologies, recur in Section I, Part III of "Notes" (C.P. 398).

jackass. She will not allow the imagination to make her lot
in life any easier. The virile youth, the hero, the poet on
horseback, descends by means of his imagination into "the
ultimate elegance: the imagined land" (C.P. 250). The figure
of the rock or the mountain occurs over and over in the
poems, but always to the same curious point. We must study
reality, the rock, the mountain, intimately, and love it so as
to come, through the imagination, to attempt to forget it and
hate it: to be gunman and lover at the same time:

> It is to disclose the essential presence, say,
> Of a mountain, expanded and elevated almost
> Into a sense, an object the less; or else
> To disclose in the figure waiting on the road
> An object the more, an undetermined form
> Between the slouchings of a gunman and a lover,
> A gesture in the dark, a fear one feels
>
> In the great vistas of night air. (C.P. 531)

That other rock, the volcano, is simply another "grey
particular of man's life," whose activity happens to vent
"evil" on man—reality in its violent aspect. The universe is
inhuman, pain is human. The escape from pain in the imaginative act is the "maximum answer" that can be truthfully
offered to the problem of evil in "Esthetique du Mal":

> The force that destroys us is disclosed, within
> This maximum, an adventure to be endured
> With the politest helplessness. Ay-mi!
> One feels its action moving in the blood. (C.P. 324)

Human desire in an inhuman universe must of necessity
promote the controlled poetic schizophrenia figured in the
lover and the gunman. One side of the mind stalks the

monster, the other seeks insatiable Florida, fears the firecat
or cherishes the cock. The beauty and horror of reality con-
vinces Stevens of the truth of evasions and the evasions of
Truth. One eats one's aspic with relish, and then meditates in
a chair in order to place oneself in the center of a diamond,
until supper time.

Chapter Four

Figures of Order

For, if we take an examination of what is
generally understood by happiness, as it has
respect either to the understanding or the
senses, we shall find all its properties and
adjuncts will herd under this short definition, that it is a perpetual possession of
being well deceived.

Jonathan Swift, *Tale of a Tub*

Nota: man is the intelligence of his soil,
The sovereign ghost. As such, the Socrates
Of snails, musician of pears, principium
And lex. Sed quaeritur: is this same wig
Of things, this nincompated pedagogue,
Preceptor to the sea? Crispin at sea
Created, in his day, a touch of doubt.
An eye most apt in gelatines and jupes,
Berries of villages, a barber's eye,
An eye of land, of simple salad-beds,
Of honest quilts, the eye of Crispin, hung
On porpoises, instead of apricots,
And on silentious porpoises, whose snouts
Dibbled in waves that were mustachios,
Inscrutable hair in an inscrutable world.[1] (C.P. 27)

---

1. For 'ghost," see § 10. The foods are all confects, delectables to
   be contrasted with the "turnip" at the end of the poem. The
   porpoise and the waves are not of the "land," Crispin's little

§ 26   Waves are mustachios only to the imaginative eye. Whether this "more than rational distortion" of reality, this "twisting," or "curling" is anything more than deception is, perhaps, impossible to decide finally in an inscrutable world. For "the very man despising honest quilts lies quilted to his poll in his despite." (C.P. 41): That is to say, even the man who despises middle-class myths ("honest quilts") can know nothing of the real world but what his "poll" or "pate" extracts from it. Hairs, and their arrangements, are seen by Stevens as the innumerable necessary deviations from reality that create an ordered imaginative "mundo."[2] The creation of mundos is not an occupation exclusive to poets; it is natural for anyone to want "a dream . . . in which I can believe in face of the object." (C.P. 174) Some dreams, however, face the object more squarely than do other dreams, some "coiffures" are more "pointed" than others. (C.P. 11) Various "barbers" and "shearsmen," imaginative people of one sort or another, clip and care for a vast assortment of wigs, pates, curls, braids and beards. Stevens exhibits his characteristic ambivalence of attitude and perspective towards all these "braidings," these orderings of reality, whether in the simplest "curl" or in the most pretentious coiffure.

In his village, Crispin felt himself the wigged judge, or lawgiver, to the world of objects. He thought his imagined universe (taken over wholesale from the transcendental imaginers of diamond-designs of the past) to be the truth about the real universe. But all these designs had their origins in the pate of Man, and whosoever considers them as the truth of things is a nincompoop. The sea, chaos of things, is

ordered world. For a full analysis of "The Comedian as the Letter C," see Chapter 9.

2.   For Stevens' attitudes toward "twists," "turns" and "curvings," see § 12.

our pedagogue, we are not its preceptor; the world is incapable of a true final ordering. The first lines then are ironic.

There is nothing much wrong with wearing a wig. One *must* have a dream in the face of the object. The inadmissible thing is to see oneself, the "guerilla I," as preceptor to the sea.

> . . . It comes to this:
> That the guerilla I should be booked
> And bound. Its nigger mystics should change
> Foolscap for wigs. Academies
> As of a tragic science should rise. (C.P. 195)

The "nigger" side of man (see § 20n.) here expends its awe in the wrong rituals, on the demands of its own desires. Wigs and foolscaps are, to be sure, both headpieces ("hats," as it were) but the former represents, in our time, a conscious distortion of the real world while the latter represents a fabrication that is simply the projection of one's ego. (There is also, probably, a pun on "foolscap," by which Stevens encourages the completely egocentric poet to stop writing till he looks about him.) One must see the real world as tragic for man. The romantic egoist with his impossible desires for personal and heavenly connections, will certainly be disillusioned and fashion his world with tragic "twists." Stevens does not ask much from the realities of life; he will accept his aloneness.

> Is it bad to have come here
> And to have found the bed empty?
>
> One might have found tragic hair,
> Bitter eyes, hands hostile and cold. (C.P. 161)

And there are consolations within this acceptance of a cold, existential life in the imagination's capacity to respond to the brilliance of natural change, and to fashion

> A poet's metaphors in which being would
>
> Come true, a point in the fire of music where
> Dazzle yields to a clarity and we observe,
>
> And observing is completing and we are content,
> In a world that shrinks to an immediate whole,
>
> That we do not need to understand, complete
> Without secret arrangements of it in the mind.
>
> There might be in the curling-out of spring
> A purple-leaping element that forth
>
> Would froth the whole heaven with its seeming-so.
>   (C.P. 341)

The passage admirably describes in metaphor the indescribable "moment" of equilibrium when the imagination's purple "curls" nature so that it is spring in its seeming so. Crispin's four saving "daughters with curls" in section VI of "The Comedian as the Letter C" are figures for various poetic kinds, different sorts of imaginings.[3] Their "curls" are neither in nature, the external world, nor wholly from the poet's self, but are products of the imaginative re-working of reality: "The relation between the imagination and reality is a question more or less of precise equilibrium" (N.A. 9). Relation is established only by "curling," and the exhausting process of constant fabrication ends only with death or with the cutting off of the poem ("clipped" has both senses):

3. See Chapter 9.

And so distorting, proving what he proves
Is nothing, what can all this matter since
The relation comes, benignly, to its end?

So may the relation of each man be clipped. (C.P. 46)

Lenin came to his end, and the "mundo" he left behind
is as unstable as the rest. The vision, the honeycomb, of any
one man cannot endure.

Go, mouse, go nibble at Lenin in his tomb.

Cut summer down to find the honey-comb.
. . . Go hunt for honey in his hair. (C.P. 217)

"Hair" is used here both as a figure for the imaginative
mundo of Lenin, and as the real thing on Lenin's head. The
sticky image of honey in his hair is purposely grotesque, so
as to point out vividly the separation of the figurative sense
of hair from hair as object. There is no real relation, the
analogy is fallacious. So, too, is the futile desire for, or ex-
pectation of, permanent answers from anyone's fiction. This
image is another example of Stevens' mixing of his metaphors with conscious purpose. He can be even more
grotesque in doing so.

When my dream was near the moon,
The white folds of its gown
Filled with yellow light.
The soles of its feet
Grew red.
Its hair filled
With certain blue crystallizations
From stars
Not far off. (C.P. 74)[4]

4. For "white" see § 14.

An imaginative Donna is suggested, but referred to as "it." This sign of disrespect to the lady is carried further by an indiscreet reference to her red feet. Now the dream's "hair" is, again, the imagination's twistings of reality (with which the soles of the fiction are in contact). But by not calling the dream "she" or "her," Stevens has not given to the "hair" of the imaginative fiction that voluptuous quality it has in: "But here is where she sat to comb her dewy hair." (C.P. 427) The attitude towards the imagination here is mixed. We have the moon, the gown, the crystallizations, and a suggestion of a woman, but she is, in one way, a gigantic curious monster. I do not assert that this particular poem is a successful attempt at conveying a mixed emotion by mixing metaphors; in fact, it seems to me uncomfortably grotesque. I bring it forward only to show how the imagination and its fictions, its curls, can be seen by Stevens from two perspectives at the same time.

§ 27   Stevens, however, in a happier mood, sees the imaginative faculty as the queen of life, whose transformations of reality mean more than the dogmas of others.

> . . . and on your head
> No crown is simpler than the simple hair.   (C.P. 87)

The crowns, the symbols of earthly (and heavenly) authority, were headpieces worn, say, by the ancient biblical patriarchs with long "beards." Beards, like hair, curls and wigs, represent transformations of reality, the product of myth-making. Stevens will sometimes use beard almost entirely in this figurative sense to represent myth, in interesting mixed metaphors like "salt masks of beard" (C.P. 101), or "gold beards of waterfalls" (O.P. 95). There have always been bearded sages (or "sculptors") engaged in myth-making,

and their beards, or world-views, are a necessary part of the
life of an age:

> The statue is the sculptor not the stone.
> In this he carved himself, he carved his age,[5]

> Ethereal compounder, pater patriae,
> Great mud-ancestor, oozer and Abraham,
> Progenitor wearing the diamond crown of crowns,
> He from whose beard the future springs, elect. (O.P. 64)

"Diamonds" and "crowns" and "Abrahams" are suspect in
our day, but the modern sage has his own beard and crown
and diamond-design, the imaginative mundo. Yet he does
not pretend to any divine illumination, divine right or heavenly hopes. He is not one of the "blessed, whose beard is
cloak against the snows" (C.P. 105).[6] There is, for Stevens,
no "father bearded in his fire" (C.P. 438) save the bearded
king (the poem or myth) that is pressed out of the imagination's will for order:

> It is clear that it is not a moral law.
> It appears to be what there is of life compressed
> Into its own illustration, a divinity
> Like any other, rex by right of the crown,
> The jewels in his beard. (O.P. 79)

From this will to transform objects into jewels comes the
bearded patriarchal form that is the fictive god of Stevens'
imaginative mundo:

> As if the crude collops came together as one,
> A mythological form, a festival sphere,
> A great bosom, beard and being, alive with age.
>
> (C.P. 466)[7]

5. For "statues" see § 29.
6. For "cloak," see § 40. Notice the mixed metaphor.
7. This form is Major Man (see § 42). For "sphere" see § 13.

Stevens has gone full circle in his festival sphere, from a denial of the pretentious bearded sages of revelation to the affirmation of an illusory bearded hero that will satisfy man's hunger for gods:

> I sing a hero's head, large eye
> And bearded bronze, but not a man,
>
> Although I patch him as I can
> And reach through him almost to man. (C.P. 165)

That his hero's head is "bronze" is enough to tell us that Stevens has, in his very moments of affirmation, something of Swift's disgust about illusion. The curls in nature we put there ourselves. The extravaganza of history exhibits the continual search for order through myth-making which comes wholly from within, the maker's myth, his beard, growing, as it were, out of his own flesh:

> Is it for nothing, then, that old Chinese
> Sat tittivating by their mountain pools
> Or in the Yangtse studied out their beards?
> I shall not play the flat historic scale.
> You know how Utamaro's beauties sought
> The end of love in their all-speaking braids.
> You know the mountainous coiffures of Bath.
> Alas! Have all the barbers lived in vain
> That not one curl in nature has survived?
> Why, without pity on these studious ghosts,
> Do you come dripping in your hair from sleep? (C.P. 14)[8]

The last two lines have given Stevens' critics a great deal of trouble, the reason being, I think, that one is always hopeful

8. For "pools," see "lakes," § 7 ; for "mountains," § 25 ; 'barbers," § 26 ; 'ghosts," "sleep," § 17. For a full analysis of "le Monocle," see Chapter 8.

of finding in Stevens a poem where dramatic characters assume more importance than their doctrinal significations. The "you" addressed is not the wife of the narrator, the middle-aged uncle; the stanza is a love ode to the "Interior Paramour," to the Imagination. From a sleep of dreams the imagination emerges with fictions that belie any absolutist's ("studious ghosts") formulation of reality, and, at the same time, declare true but irrelevant Swift's satirical observation that all pleasing images are deception.[9] The Imagination bathes her hair in Reality's mountain pool, and orders the world as inevitably as season follows season:

> In the green water, clear and warm,
> Susanna lay.
> She searched
> The touch of springs,
> And found
> Concealed imaginings.
> She sighed,
> For so much melody.
>
> Upon the bank, she stood
> In the cool
> Of spent emotions. (C.P. 90)

In and out of the water, in summer and in autumn, the imagination finds, the imagination spends. Fictional Susannas die, as the mind destroys all "romantic tenements" of rose and ice, only to raise them up again.

9. Prof. Arthur Mizener has written to me of these lines: "The expression 'in your hair' traditionally means 'with your hair hanging free and naturally.' Virgins were married 'in their hair'; others with their hair 'up'."
Utamaro's beauties braided their hair up into mountainous coiffures. The modern imagination is pristine in its purity and its poverty.

§ 28 Building up and tearing down, creating and destroying, continual love and strife is the occupation of the mind. The human imagination, part of the mind, constructs "tenements" or artifacts which represent an ordering of an age. There is in Stevens a large assemblage of figures of artifacts, artifacts of a period or a place which represent an attitude or posture towards reality that was prevalent in that age, that place. Many of these are wholly accessible to the casual reader, say the steeple, the chariot, carriage and motor car, the tambourine, banjo or tin can, etc. Some others are not so obvious in their signification when seen with Stevens' equivocal eye.

We have seen how the figure of the natural diamond is used by Stevens to represent a false ordering of reality, the universe in a supposedly natural, immortal diamond-design. But there is also, in Stevens' double vision, the cut, the fashioned diamond that embellishes the "hair" of women, or their fans:

> How explicit the coiffures became,
> The diamond point, the sapphire point,
> The sequins
> Of the civil fans!   (C.P. 11)

Diamonds here represent those dazzling insights, flashes of metaphor, that go into the making up of a poetic myth (the "coiffure" or the "civil fan"). The coiffures become "explicit" in the moonlight of the imaginative dream. These fictive diamonds are often set together in a "crown," the complete fiction. Any crown fashioned for reality must be wrought with the minimum of distortion, "the slightest crown of Gothic prong" (C.P. 295) One wants to project neither pure idea (the abstraction) nor pure "thing" (the object), neither

a crown without Mrs. Pappadopoulos, nor Mrs. Pappadopoulos without her crown:

> . . . She floats in the contention, the flux
> Between the thing as idea and
> The idea as thing. (C.P. 295)

Contention, constant war, is the necessary mental state of
the artist. Any order made, the "sculpture," cannot pretend
to the reality that is Mrs. Pappalopoulos:

> The arrangement contains the desire of
> The artist. But one confides in what has no
> Concealed creator. One walks easily
>
> The unpainted shore, accepts the world
> As anything but sculpture. Good-bye,
> Mrs. Pappadopoulos, and thanks. (C.P. 296)

§ 29   Behind all "sculpture" (the work of "hands"[10]),
behind all the artistic achievement is the concealed creator
and his desire. The "statue" which rose out of the artist's

---

10. Earlier (§ 7) we mentioned that "hand" is a figure for the projection of the self, drawn by the will to make gestures, gestures
towards order:

> Working, with big hands, on the town,
> Arranging its heroic attitudes. (C.P. 227)

The imagination ("her," below), arranging objects, creates a
mundo (the garden) in the mind which represents the only
possible union between the self "him," the "mi-bird") and
objects. This fictive union is figured as a hand clasp:

> Her hand took his and drew him near to her
> Her hair fell on him and the mi-bird flew
> To the ruddier bushes at the garden's end. (C.P. 271)

(See further C.P. 306, O.P. 43, O.P. 80).

war with meaninglessness lends value to life for a while, and then is meaningless to another age:

> Even imagination has an end,
> When the statue is not a thing imagined, a stone
> That changed in sleep. It is, it is, let be
> The way it came, let be what it may become. (O. P. 71)

This is the summation passage at the end of "Owl's Clover." The whole of this long poem presents a confused, complex surface which is in part due to the very real tensions, to Stevens' mixed feelings about the necessary destruction of the artifacts of the past, present and future. The grand and the grandiose, it seemed to him, must both be sacrificed. Crows "anoint" the statues, and mice run between equestrian legs. The noble gestures of the past have hardly any meaning in the twentieth century; bronze and marble imply a fixed and permanent order of which men can know nothing. Reality (the sun) is no "sculptor" for man's spirit, for its hunger for permanence:

> Sun is
> A monster-maker, an eye, only an eye,
> A shapener of shapes for only the eye,
> Of things no better than paper things, of days
> That are paper days. The false and true are one.
>   (C.P. 252–3)

§ 30   Men like Crispin started out as romantics, but after standing in the "sun" too long changed their idea of it, and of themselves:

>   . . . nothing of himself
> Remained, except some starker, barer self
> In a starker, barer world, in which the sun

Was not the sun because it never shone
With bland complaisance on pale parasols,
Beetled, in chapels, on the chaste bouquets. (C.P. 29)

It is chaste, sentimental ordering that arranges "bouquets"
in bowls and jars, that holds a "parasol" to keep the full
strength of the sun from itself. Even poets use parasols:

Eulalia ["Fair Speech"], I lounged on the hospital porch,
On the east, sister and nun, and opened wide
a parasol, which I had found, against
The sun. The interior of a parasol,
It is a kind of blank in which one sees. (C.P. 287)

Even Hartford, Conn., can be seen imaginatively under a
"purple" parasol:

What is this purple, this parasol,
This stage-light of the Opera?
It is like a region full of intonings.
It is a Hartford seen in a purple light. (C.P. 226)[11]

§ 31   All arrangements, then, coiffures, crowns, sculp-
tures, bouquets and parasols, etc., are false, though some
are more false than others. Falseness is of necessity bred
within the mind by the hunger for permanence. We take a
part of reality and treat it for a while as the whole. This
"part" is neither an Eden nor a medieval garden. We have
no divine spot or zone in some great hierarchy of being. We
live in a "park," a park whose boundaries are, partly, the
limitations of our minds, partly the fences we fabricate to
allow within just so much of reality as we can order and

11. "Opera" because the imagination makes a theatrical ordering.
Stevens is being ironic again about the poet's business. For
"theatre," see § 32.

endure. The boundaries are flexible but always there. Within the park is the "mansion" in which we live, the "theatre" in which we play a part, the plants and animals and objects which we twist to our liking. The imaginative man seeks for "portals" and "foyers" at the outer boundaries of the park, and perhaps finds them. But then the park extends to envelop these. And the final truth is: "We live in a camp . . . Stanzas of final peace lie in the heart's residium . . .Amen." (C.P. 258) Life is seen as an armed camp where only the mind (or "heart"), tired from constant war against chaos, can summon up a moment's peace. This is, in brief, the real world of the twentieth-century poet as seen by Stevens. To know Stevens, his vision, and the tonality of his mind, we need to look at this world of parks more closely.

The park with the most limited boundaries is that of the masses in "Owl's Clover":

> The workers do not rise, as Venus rose,
> Out of a violet sea. They rise a bit
> On summer Sundays in the park . . .
>
> They rise to the muddy, metropolitan elms,
> To the camellia-chateaux and an inch beyond.   (O.P. 60)

The masses will listen to any "architect," live in any park given to them, whether by leaders of the present or "skeletons" from the past:

> These bands, these swarms, these motions, what of them?
> They keep to the paths of the skeleton architect
> Of the park. They obey the rules of every skeleton.
>
> (O.P. 62)

All parks of the past were fictions that passed in time, and we must live, disenchanted, in a modern park:

> The envoi to the past
> Is largely another winding of the clock.
> The tempo, in short, of the complicated shift . . .
> The summer Sundays in the park, must be
> A leaden ticking circular in width.
> How shall we face the edge of time? We walk
> In the park. We regret we have no nightingale.
> We must have the throstle on the gramophone. (O.P. 66)

The figure here is of the pernicious circle again (§ 13). The transcendent imaginers of the past (who heard the "nightingale") had pretentions to final truth; the poet who believes neither in transcendence nor in final truth, must ever face self-derision at the close of his own hymns, as Stevens, listening to the throstle on the gramophone.

Stevens faces this situation in two ways. He can focus on the center of the park, the human comedy, the local environment, or he can seek for "things dark on the horizons of perception" (C.P. 508). The poet can focus on his "mansion" in the park, and make poems of it that become part of what the mansion is:

> . . . Children,
> Still weaving budded aureoles,
> Will speak our speech and never know,
> Will say of the mansion that it seems
> As if he that lived there left behind
> A spirit storming in blank walls,
> A dirty house in a gutted world. (C.P. 159)[12]

Crispin, at first, was like the children and did not realize what sort of place he lived in,

12. "Aureole" the mystic's crown, to be contrasted with the imaginative crown. See § 28. For "walls" and "house," see § 7.

> . . . he that saw
> The stride of vanishing autumn in a park
> By way of decorous melancholy.   (C.P. 31)

The mature vision of the human comedy as Stevens sees it is brilliantly projected in the lines, "Life is an old casino in the park," a casino with rain sweeping through its boarded windows and leaves falling into its encrusted fountains.[13] And the older the poet gets, the less the human comedy in the park amuses him, till finally his vision of the exterior world is of a nothingness, a "vacancy in the park" where:

> The four winds blow through the rustic arbor,
> Under its mattresses of vines.   (C.P. 511)

The living vines, sometime figures for an ordered, fruitful reality, here are seen as mattresses, where the people are sleeping as the poet is, in a subjective phantasma.

§ 32   Another figure for the interior of the park is the "theatre." The old theatre, the old order is gone:

> A tempest cracked in the theatre. Quickly,
> The wind beat in the roof and half the walls.
> The ruin stood still in an external world.
> It had been real.
>
> The people sat in the theatre, in the ruin,
> As if nothing had happened.
>
> It was a blue scene washing white in the rain.   (C.P. 306)

The modern theatre is "bare board" and bricks, "without scenery or lights" (C.P. 427). Tragic gesticulation towards "theatrical distances" (C.P. 129) does one little good. What

13. For "leaves," see § 38.

is needed is a new myth, a new theatre, and the mind must construct it. It must declaim to itself ("The poet represents the mind in the act of defending us against itself"), hoping through speech to unite two disparate feelings towards its situation:

      . . . It has
To construct a new stage. It has to be on that stage
And, like an insatiable actor, slowly and
With meditation, speak words that in the ear,
In the delicatest ear of the mind, repeat,
Exactly, that which it wants to hear, at the sound
Of which, an invisible audience listens,
Not to the play, but to itself, expressed
In an emotion as of two people, as of two
Emotions becoming one. (C.P. 240)

§ 33   But these new myths that Stevens calls for are not myths that will ever again unite the whole world of people and things. These myths are obviously personal; each man must be his own myth-maker. The impulse is towards a retreat inwards, to the very center of the self, and at the same time towards a flight outwards beyond the theatre, the mansions, the park, beyond the "last thought" (O.P. 117) to the edge of space. What Stevens wishes to find there is not obvious. Partly, as a poet in control of his doctrines, he wants the maximum exploration of the "park,"

                . . . the mind,
The starting point of the human and the end,
That in which space itself is contained, the gate
To the enclosure, day, the things illumined

By day, night and that which night illumines,

Night and its midnight-minting fragrances,
Night's hymn of the rock, as in a vivid sleep.   (C.P. 528)[14]

But, as Mr. R. P. Blackmur points out, the doctrine in Stevens is not usually in control; we are dealing with a "sensibility in desperation" where "statements come out as lyric cries all the more moving because we feel in them a craving for a fuller being than they can ever reach."[15] There is in Stevens a desire to transcend the park, to pass through the "portal" that leads not to a "foyer" of another theatre of an age, but to a foyer of the spirit, or the soul, to an absolute foyer. He always denies the wish immediately; there is no absolute foyer, he says, only the resting places, the "moments," those imaginative integrations of common things within the park:

He knew that he was a spirit without a foyer
And that, in his knowledge, local objects become
More precious than the most precious objects of home:

The local objects of a world without a foyer,
Without a remembered past, a present past,
Or a present future, hoped for in present hope,

Objects not present as a matter of course
On the dark side of the heavens or the bright,
In that sphere with so few objects of its own.

Little existed for him but the few things
For which a fresh name always occurred, as if
He wanted to make them, keep them from perishing,

14. "Day" represents phenomena unabstracted; "night" represents phenomena seen in the moonlight of the imagination. The "enclosure" of course is the mind. For "Rock" see § 25.
15. Blackmur, p. 222.

The few things, the objects of insight, the integrations
Of feeling, the things that came of their own accord,
Because he desired without knowing quite what,

That were the moments of the classic, the beautiful.
These were that serene he had always been approaching
As toward an absolute foyer beyond romance.

(O.P. 111–112)

The position is a nominalist one. The second and third
stanzas by their very syntax, by their reiteration of what the
objects are not, carry the submerged desire that they could
be more than they are. The objects are objects seen by the
imagination, insights, integrations, that do not come as a
matter of course, and, alas, do not stay "in that sphere," the
mind. The serenity they bring him in moments of equilibrium
has its pathos since the moments are *as* an absolute foyer,
though they are no such thing:[16] "the crows are flying above
the foyer of summer" (C.P. 457). There is no final "summer"
free of squawking "crows." Man must always return to, and
end in, the foyer of winter, "the late, least foyer in a qualm
of cold" (C.P. 457).

Stevens consistently shows an understanding of, almost a
longing for religious belief, for a transcendent paradise
"beyond" phenomena. He has no patience with the people
who are certain that Reason and Humanism can carry one

16. "As" and "beyond" are intentionally slippery words in Stevens.
The whole problem of analogic fallacy which gives Stevens'
poems their odd tonality is the problem of "as." And how one
goes "beyond" things is a central crux in Stevens. A fictive
mundo can be beyond reality through distortion, through new
meaningful integration, or through transcendence. Stevens' Will
and Desire long for transcendence; in his "moments" Stevens
feels his integrations are meaningful; in his rational moments
he fears he has done nothing but distort, since "as" is not "is"
in any meaningful way.

to a foyer of the spirit where either the religious or the aesthetic imagination is no longer necessary, where thought satisfies desire. The truth is that reason can make no important connections, no analogies that are vital to the spirit. It is better then to create limited myths out of local objects than to have any faith in the rationalist's crude foyer:

> Thought is false happiness: the idea
> That merely by thinking one can,
> Or may, penetrate, not may,
> But can, that one is sure to be able—
>
> That there lies at the end of thought
> A foyer of the spirit in a landscape
> Of the mind, in which we sit
> And wear humanity's bleak crown;
>
> In which we read the critique of paradise
> And say it is the work
> Of a comedian, this critique;
> In which we sit and breathe
>
> An innocence of an absolute,
> False happiness, since we know that we use
> Only the eye as faculty, that the mind
> Is the eye, and that this landscape of the mind
>
> Is a landscape only of the eye; and that
> We are ignorant men incapable
> Of the least, minor, vital metaphor, content,
> At last, there, when it turns out to be here. (C.P. 305)

§ 34   The only approach to a foyer outside of the park that we can hope for is that of the classical, the beautiful, the serene aesthetic moment:

Beauty is momentary in the mind—
The fitful tracing of a portal. (C.P. 91)

As more of reality comes under the poet's fitful command,
he sees the portal at the vast end of the park:

> Ramon Fernandez, tell me, if you know,
> Why, when the singing ended and we turned
> Toward the town, tell why the glassy lights,
> The lights in the fishing boats at anchor there,
> As the night descended, tilting in the air,
> Mastered the night and portioned out the sea,
> Fixing emblazoned zones and fiery poles,
> Arranging, deepening, enchanting night.
>
> Oh! Blessed rage for order, pale Ramon,
> The maker's rage to order words of the sea,
> Words of the fragrant portals, dimly-starred. (C.P. 130)

In that time of equilibrium it is as if there were an "angel
of reality standing at the door" (C.P. 496), bidding the poet
to come to the "threshold" (see C.P. 511) and there, beyond
reason, to behold for a moment a vision of an aesthetic
order, permanent within flux, a foyer in which he, happy
nonetheless, has no permanent place:

> The palm at the end of the mind,
> Beyond the last thought, rises
> In the bronze distance,
>
> A gold-feathered bird
> Sings in the palm, without human meaning,
> Without human feeling, a foreign song.
>
> You know then that it is not the reason
> That makes us happy or unhappy.
> The bird sings. Its feathers shine.

> The palm stands on the edge of space.
> The wind moves slowly in the branches.
> The bird's fire-fangled feathers dangle down.[17]

(O.P. 117–18)

This exquisite poem, "Of Mere Being," is one of the last poems Stevens wrote, and is a pure distillation of much of what he has to say. Figures here take on the depth of symbols, and Stevens' double vision toward his figures comes to a single focus so that we feel for once the tranquil equilibrium Stevens writes about, rather than the tension characteristic of his poems. The poem cannot be completely handled here. The wind and the fire, the slow-motion and the "dangling" are best dealt with elsewhere (see § 44). The central figures, however, the palm and the bird, its song and feathers, are figures of order within the park. We must come to their meaning now by a twisting route.

§ 35

> Postpone the anatomy of summer, as
> The physical pine, the metaphysical pine.
> Let's see the very thing and nothing else.   (C.P. 373)

The mood of "summer" (§ 16), if anatomized, will show that a real object, say a pine tree, takes on accretions and significations that have to do with the poet's subjective desires, so that the pine finally has a place in doctrine that has little to do with the facts of that particular tree.

The "red" fern (see § 14) represents an object in reality difficult to fix in our perception because the mind abstracts from reality (the "physical") in the moment of looking:

17. Note the contrast of bronze and "gold": bronze is reality's cold permanence, gold is the imagination's order, a fictive permanence.

The large-leaved day grows rapidly,
And opens in this familiar spot
Its unfamiliar, difficult fern,
Pushing and pushing red after red. (C.P. 365)

The leaves are the green and familiar and omnipresent
(though still "large," still a projection of the mind; see § 38),
in contrast to the unfamiliar red fern. The red fern is, however, in fact, the closest "relation to the parent trunk, the
dazzling, bulging, brightest core, the furiously burning
father fire," or reality apart from man's cloudy perception of
it. An "infant" (C.P. 462), who can only ask "What is that?"
is dumbfounded by a simple object, the fern itself. Old men,
for whom "everything is psychic" are dumbfounded by the
fern's existence, its metaphysical cause:

Infant, it is enough in life
To speak of what you see. But wait
Until sight wakens the sleepy eye
And pierces the physical fix of things. (C.P. 365)

Such an old man, finally, lies "deep in the grass of sleep, deep
grass that totters under the weight of light" (O.P. 54–5). He
has created his own subjective mundo in the real green grass
where he lies until the "dinner bell" (like the cocks crow,
§ 19) rings in the real world, "in the green, outside the door
of phantasm" (O.P. 110). There is no doubt, "he was facing
phantasma when the bell rang." Such a complete withdrawal
into the subjective self is, finally, a bad thing for Stevens. He
must live with both the metaphysical pine and the physical
pine around him, skirting both phantasm and the "prerogative jumble" (N.A. 84). The "blue-green" pines (C.P. 191)
must be "a little changed by tips of artifice" (C.P. 350), but
they must remain essentially what they are, say, "appala-
chian" pines (see C.P. 76).

§ 36   The serpent in the fern (C.P. 411) is one of Stevens' most effective figures for this duality with which man is faced. The serpent is half real animal, strange, beautiful and poisonous, half symbol for the creative act, the sinuous weaving and twisting through reality, catching the sunflash, glittering, ever-changing (shedding its skin), winding up-wardly to a "new nest" that it will never find till it reaches death, the "black sublime" (see O.P. 55). The upward wind-ing means everything to Stevens, and yet he can see the creation is "bodiless," "air," ending in "formlessness" and "disbelief" (allowing for the ambiguity in these words):

> This is where the serpent lives, the bodiless.
> His head is air.
>
> This is where the serpent lives. This is his nest,
> These fields, these hills, these tinted distances,
> And the pines above and along and beside the sea.
>
> This is form gulping after formlessness,
> Skin flashing to wished-for disappearances
> And the serpent body flashing without the skin.
>
> This is the height emerging and its base
> These lights may finally attain a pole
> In the midmost midnight and find the serpent there,
>
> In another nest, the master of the maze
> Of body and air and forms and images,
> Relentlessly in possession of happiness.
>
> This is his poison: that we should disbelieve
> Even that.   (C.P. 411)

The will impels us to the search for a foyer further than that we have reached, though we well know the doubleness of what we will find there:

The possible nest in the invisible tree,
Which in a composite season, now unknown,
Denied, dismissed, may hold a serpent, loud
In our captious hymns, erect and sinuous,
Whose venom and whose wisdom will be one. (C.P. 437)[18]

§ 37   The palm is, too, a slippery figure. Stevens makes use of the various traditional and archetypal palms. There is the palm of religious ritual, the palm as reward for victory in competition, and the palm as exotic plant of the southern isles. In Stevens' comic ironic eye, the palm can mean an absurd desire for tropical ease or for divine reward. In Stevens' serious eye, the palm as metaphysical palm, can represent, like the fern, the desire to pierce the "physical fix of things," to go beyond phenomena to some knowledge of what philosophy calls the noumena. Or the palm can be a figure for the aesthetic mundo that serves the poet, however unsatisfactorily, as his only analogy to the incomprehensible, inexpressible noumena.[19]

18. The passage expresses the hope of "St. John," a figure for the doctrinal side of Stevens' mind. His "backache," a figure for his ironic side, is dubious of ever bridging the abyss, finding the nest.

19. Kant's symbol for the noumena is X. Stevens undoubtedly was aware of this, but his use of X is, it seems to me, more limited. X is any formulation (by transference, the formulator) of reality, of chaos. One must be ready to discard one's formulations. X, finally, "is an obstruction" (see C.P. 310). In the "Anecdote of Canna," X, the mighty thought, must be changed as the poet's perception of the simple flower changes (C.P. 55). The poet, of course, formulates; it is only human to want to know and speak of the noumena. But his statements will only be "effective," not "true," and Stevens is honest about this. X for the poet is a formulation, but a metaphoric formulation, engaging, but partaking completely of analogic fallacy, the poet
     Desiring the exhilarations of changes:
     The motive for metaphor, shrinking from
     The weight of primary noon,
     The A B C of being,   [cont'd. on p. 84]

> Barque of phosphor
> On the palmy beach,
> Move outward into heaven. (C.P. 23)

The "heaven" is of the "night blues" and the "moonlight,"
that make a "barque of phosphor" out of one's "black hull,"
one's real life (see C.P. 23). One is exhorted to sail into a
transient imaginative mundo, where, finally, the clarity of
an order *obscures* the physical palm:

> Say that the palms are clear in the total blue,
> Are clear and are obscure; that it is night;
> That the moon shines. (C.P. 86)

The palms in the two passages following clearly are "metaphysical" palms, representing false orders that satisfy or
have satisfied:

> There is not any haunt of prophecy,
> Nor any old chimera of the grave,
> Neither the golden underground, nor isle
> Melodious, where spirits gat them home,
> Nor visionary south, nor cloudy palm
> Remote on heaven's hill, that has endured
> As April's green endures. (C.P. 68)

> Take the moral law and make a nave of it
> And from the nave build haunted heaven. Thus,
> The conscience is converted into palms,
> Like windy citherns hankering for hymns.
> We agree in principle. That's clear. But take

> The ruddy temper, the hammer
> Of red and blue, the hard sound—
> Steel against intimation—the sharp flash,
> The vital, arrogant, fatal, dominant X. (C.P. 288)
> The real X, Kant's X, cannot be formulated.

The opposing law and make a peristyle,
And from the peristyle project a masque
Beyond the planets. Thus, our bawdiness,
Unpurged by epitaph, indulged at last,
Is equally converted into palms. (C.P. 59)

As the formulations about gods have no basis, neither do
romantic statements about the nature and destiny of man.
The poetic hero comes "without palms or jugglery" (C.P.
35). The poet must cultivate his own "palms" that "shall
tuft the commonplace" (O.P. 17), palms that in the poet's
fictions will "rise up beyond the sea" (C.P. 344), make an
order out of the chaos of perception, a palm at the "end of
the mind" (O.P. 117).

§ 38   Leaves are green, familiar, and infinitely numerous
objects in a spring and summer reality. Trees are leafless in
the November blackness; they fall in the autumn of the year
and of a poet's life. From these familiar observations concerning seasonal change and mortal decay, Stevens constructs
a simple drama that has to do with the mind's transient
moods and the cyclical permanence of imaginative acts.

"For myself, I live by leaves" (C.P. 134), Stevens as
"botanist" says; what does he mean? His search is always
for the "new leaf" (C.P. 21), a new way of seeing objects in
the park, as in the summer time when the "leaves rattled their
gold" (C.P. 222), or in winter, "in the sound of a few leaves"
(C.P. 10), or in extreme old age when one approaches "total
leaflessness" (C.P. 477). The mind and its environment of
objects (leaves) together create ever-fluctuating moods in the
aging poet, who can expect no return of green, but only a
slow domination of black. As the falling leaves represent
beauty or youth passing, they can represent the words of
poetry which create "gardens" (which, too, pass). It is said

in "Sunday Morning" that our hunger for beauty in our mortal lives causes

> . . . boys to pile new plums and pears
> On disregarded plate. The maidens taste
> And stray impassioned in the littering leaves.[20]
>
> (C.P. 69)

The plums and pears figure the poet's fictions; the maidens figure our desire for beauty. Ultimately the fruits go stale, the fiction is disregarded, the "leaves" are littered in the garden.

Thus in Stevens, the physical leaves are figures for these blessed thoughts, or integrations which, expressed in the words of poetry, keep one's mind from the void:

> The mobile and the immobile flickering
> In the area between is and was are leaves,
> Leaves burnished in autumnal burnished trees
>
> And leaves in whirlings in the gutters, whirlings
> Around and away, resembling the presence of thought,
> Resembling the presences of thoughts, as if,
>
> In the end, in the whole psychology, the self,
> The town, the weather, in a casual litter,
> Together, said words of the world are the life of the world.
>
> (C.P. 474)

20. 'Sunday Morning" was originally published in *Poetry* (1915) in five stanzas (stanzas I, VIII, IV, V, VII of the version in *Collected Poems*) and only these lines differ:

> . . . boys to bring sweet-smelling pears
> And plums in ponderous piles. The maidens taste

The "disregarded plate" of the final version adds, I think to the poignancy of the poem. But I must confess that the three added stanzas and the rearranging of the stanzas seem to me to detract from the honesty of the original and cover the poem with a romantic haze.

Leaves, then, are both objects and words. The words of man, ordered in poetry, come infinitely and go infinitely, as particulars, but endure as an answer in general:

> . . . an illusion so desired
> That the green leaves came and covered the high rock,
> That the lilacs came and bloomed, like a blindness cleaned,
> Exclaiming bright sight, as it was satisfied,
>
> In a birth of sight. The blooming and the musk
> Were being alive, an incessant being alive,
> A particular of being, that gross universe.
>
> The fiction of the leaves is the icon
>
> Of the poem, the figuration of blessedness,
> And the icon is the man. The pearled chaplet of spring,
> The magnum wreath of summer, time's autumn snood,
>
> Its copy of the sun, these cover the rock.
> These leaves are the poem, the icon and the man.
> These are a cure of the ground and of ourselves,
>
> In the predicate that there is nothing else.
> They bud and bloom and bear their fruit without change.
> They are more than leaves that cover the barren rock
>
> They bud the whitest eye, the pallidest sprout,
> New senses in the engenderings of sense,
> The desire to be at the end of distances. (C.P. 526–7)

§ 39 The physical leaves fall, and the black hemlock alone looms large in the landscape (C.P. 8). But the memory of the joy of words, of "leaves" in summer and of the peacock's cry (and the splendor of his tail) ward off the blackness of night:

> At night, by the fire,
> The colors of the bushes
> And of the fallen leaves,
> Repeating themselves,
> Turned in the room,
> Like the leaves themselves
> Turning in the wind.
> Yes: but the color of the heavy hemlocks
> Came striding.
> And I remembered the cry of the peacocks.

The peacock's cry may be felt as a cry against the twilight, or the hemlock, or the falling of the leaves, or all of these together, a cry of fear or of loss. The brilliantly colored and patterned tail of the peacock, like the panache of forms in the parakeet's tail (see C.P. 82), represents the gaudium of natural forms. The flight of the peacock from the bough of the hemlock represents the life that is ordered motion, the beautiful, balanced, curved arc, the imaginative equilibrium between the sharp, straight lines of reality and the closed circle of the ultimate intellect. The aesthetic ordering takes place, to be sure, in the bleak atmosphere of a turning world, blown by winds of change and mortal fears:

> And I remembered the cry of the peacocks.

> The colors of their tails
> Were like the leaves themselves
> Turning in the wind,
> In the twilight wind.
> They swept over the room,
> Just as they flew from the boughs of the hemlocks
> Down to the ground.
> I heard them cry—the peacocks.
> Was it a cry against the twilight

Or against the leaves themselves
Turning in the wind. (C.P. 8–9)

The cry of the birds in the park and their flights are figures
of order. The plumage of a bird, feathers and tail, represent
the perceptions of varying forms and colors the imagination
draws upon for new orderings. Any given integration of
these forms must be discarded with every new springtime;
last year's cock turns "white," and a new bird is ready in
the imagination.

The white cock's tail
Tosses in the wind.
The turkey-cock's tail
Glitters in the sun. (C.P. 20)[21]

The "gold-feathered" bird (O.P. 117 and § 34), however,
is not intended by Stevens to be another "bird of mutable
plume" (C.P. 348). It is a projection of a desire to escape the
sun's bronze (time); it is "fire-fangled," created to withstand
the ravishes of the (Heracleitean) fire, which consumes all
objects of reality. Such a bird is conceived in the imaginative
eye; it is never to be perceived in the ocean of phenomena:

The generations of the bird are all
By water washed away. They follow after.
They follow, follow, follow, in water washed away.

Without this bird that never settles, without

21. There may be, in addition, in this poem, "Ploughing on
Sunday," a hint of the white dove of Christianity in the white
cock. The old myth is dead, the poet ploughs North America
("local objects") on "Sunday," the old day of rest. I offer this as
mere conjecture, but see, for example, the white swans in
"Invective against Swans" and in "Academic Discourse," which
are definitely figures for the Christian myths.

> Its generations that follow in their universe,
> The ocean, falling and falling on the hollow shore,
>
> Would be a geography of the dead.   (C.P. 304)

These birds never settle on a bough. They are figures for the imaginative aspect of the mind ever creating, ever destroying, evading deadly repose in its fictions ("ripenings") or in hollow reality (the "point" of redness).

> The sun is the country wherever he is. The bird
> In the brightest landscape downwardly revolves
> Disdaining each astringent ripening,
> Evading the point of redness, not content
> To repose in an hour or season or long era
> Of the country colors crowding against it, since
> The yellow grassman's mind is still immense,
> Still promises perfections cast away.   (C.P. 318)

The mind's eye of the poet, the yellow grassman, perceives nature (the green grass) in the yellow light of the sun. Nature, the sun's country, is not enough for the poet; he desires the "further consummation," an ordering, a "transmutation which, when seen, appears to be askew" (C.P. 318). The "big bird" in this poem, which pecks on the poet with insatiable appetite, is the mind and its "rage for order."

The bird that can no longer fly is a fiction that no longer suffices:

> A blue pigeon it is, that circles the blue sky,
> On sidelong wing, around and round and round.
> A white pigeon it is, that flutters to the ground,
> Grown tired of flight.   (C.P. 17)

The flight of the birds is, however, a slow curve downwards,

as day falls into night, sunlight to darkness, life to death,
the imagination's summer to late autumn:

> And, in the isolation of the sky,
> At evening, casual flocks of pigeons make
> Ambiguous undulations as they sink,
> Downward to darkness, on extended wings. (C.P. 70)

They sink bearing no divine message, as the dove did: the
beauty in the lazy circling (in summer) and the down descent
(in November) is always ambiguous, mixed with the isolation, the terror of the darkness. The response to flights of
such beauty, such terror, such ambiguity, comes not from
the rational man within us, but directly from the "subman"
the "nigger self" (see § 20) who can innocently feel awe at
natural beauty, and who can twist imaginative kinks from
the sun-dazzle:

> Tell me more of the eagle, Cotton,
> And you, black Sly,
> Tell me how he descended
> Out of the morning sky.
>
> Describe with deepened voice
> And noble imagery
> His slowly-falling round
> Down to the fishy sea.
>
> Here was a sovereign sight,
> Fit for a kinky clan.
> Tell me again of the point
> At which the flight began,
>
> Say how his heavy wings,
> Spread on the sun-bronzed air,
> Turned tip and tip away,
> Down to the sand, the glare

> Of the pine trees edging the sand,
> Dropping in sovereign rings
> Out of his fiery lair
> Speak of the dazzling wings. (C.P. 126–127)

The bird figure here has come full circle. The sun teaches us all we know, all we can perceive, and out of the sun's arrangements we fashion imaginative birds. Here the eagle figure is actually projecting the rise, zenith and descent of the sun. Its "nigger mystics" watch the natural process with natural reverence. The twisting flight of the imagination occurs when things and their natural motion are slightly "tipped," and seen then as "bright discursive wings" (C.P. 243).

The imagination is a "bird of intermitted bliss singing in the night's abyss" (O.P. 4). Or, the imagination is "the desired, listening to the birds who sing" without human meaning "beyond the last thought."

> She attends the tintinnabula
>
> Of birds called up by more than the sun,
> Birds of more wit, that substitute
>
> Their intelligible twittering
> For unintelligible thought. (C.P. 505)

The birds are more than sun, more than real birds; will and desire have made them so. It is desire (in what Stevens calls the "soul") for permanence, for an absolute foyer, that flies beyond the parks, beyond the flux of phenomena, beyond "listless" (Christian) myths, and man's inflated conceptions of himself:

> The soul, O ganders, flies beyond the parks
> And far beyond the discords of the wind.

A bronze rain from the sun descending marks
The death of summer, which that time endures

Like one who scrawls a listless testament
Of golden quirks and Paphian caricatures,

Bequeathing your white feathers to the moon
And giving your bland motions to the air.

Behold, already on the long parades
The crows anoint the statues with their dirt.

And the soul, O ganders, being lonely, flies
Beyond your chilly chariots, to the skies.   (C.P. 4)[22]

The "soul," we shall have occasion to see, cannot really
escape the discords of the wind and air (see § 44), and what
it will find in the skies will be, consistently, that "dividing
and indifferent blue" (C.P. 68). But the bird must never
settle lest it fall in the ocean, "the geography of the dead."

§ 40   Man then must constantly live within some myth
or other; artifacts like the statue in the park or the poem
about a bird in flight make an order out of phenomena for
an age or for a certain sensibility. But even more important
than the ordering of the external world is the composing of a
self. The bronze rain from the sun has stripped man naked in
our time; he is without an absolute belief, or absolute values,
or a central noble position in the world.

22. The "which" in line 4 refers to "summer." The summer mood
must yield to autumn, like the New Testament writer who
scrawls "quirks" and "caricatures" of holy writ long after the
time of revelation. The white-feathered ganders and the chilly
chariots are Christian references. The bronze rain is washing out
all these old fictions.

The mordant side of Stevens' mind cherishes, demands, "nakedness," wishes the object and the self absolutely stripped of all metaphorical accretions. But nakedness itself has, too, to be imagined:

> But nakedness, wollen massa, concerns an innermost atom.
> If that remains concealed, what does the bottom matter?
> (C.P. 145)

The paltry Nude (C.P. 5) is skimming the "spick" torrent without the attendants that Venus had. She is, in fact, reality figured as a woman. And she,

> . . . She too is discontent
> And would have purple stuff upon her arms. (C.P. 5)

Stevens implores that other female figure of reality, Florida, his insatiable mistress, "venereal soil," to come to him in the weavings of the imagination:

> Donna, donna, dark,
> Stooping in indigo gown
> And cloudy constellations,
> Conceal yourself or disclose
> Fewest things to the lover—
> A hand that bears a thick-leaved fruit,
> A pungent bloom against your shade. (C.P. 48)

Reality, without the draping of the indigo gown, is not bearable. One selects from reality's objects (the fruit, the bloom) those which please the imagination and "clothes" the object by the imaginative "hand." The poet must make "silk dresses out of worms" (O.P. 157), grow a "beard" that is "cloak against the snows" (C.P. 105). Nakedness (the casting off of old beliefs) is but a necessary stage to a modern mythology of the self. The poet must look within, and not

to old mythologies, draperies of old orders. He must drop
"the cloak and speech of Virgil" (C.P. 185).

Crispin in his early salad days in the villages was a motley,
accepted the trappings of past civilizations though there is no
body of reality to inform them:

Crispin,

The ribboned stick, the bellowing breeches, cloak
Of China, cap of Spain, imperative haw
Of hum.   (C.P. 28)

Stevens sees relation between body and spirit in an interesting way. Our bodies are "animal," but the animal contains
the "anima," the spirit, the imaginative faculty, which
"weaves" our *raisons d'etre,* the robes, caps, cloaks, and
other clothes in which we endure. So spirit informs our trappings as our bodies, and both are subject to decay. We are
but "bellowing breeches" if we turn our eyes away from
reality towards an old mythology. The sea, chaotic reality, is
incapable of being ordered, "formed to mind or voice," and
so is "wholly body" (C.P. 128). Any myth woven around the
sea will be simply a curious cloak, "fluttering its empty
sleeves," since the body of truth will not be in it. No body,
no spirit; no spirit, no body.

It gets difficult to clothe ourselves. Penelope, waiting,
weaves her cretonnes (C.P. 520), the old poet wraps about
him a single shawl (C.P. 524). "Weaker and weaker the sunlight falls in the afternoon" (C.P. 504), till finally, in the
"indigence of the light," a "stellar pallor hangs upon the
threads." The old fictions do not color life anymore. The
sun, when it is strong, and the self, when it is likewise,
together weave the "angel" of reality (the Fiction), who
describes himself as

> . . . an apparition apparelled in
> Apparels of such lightest look that a turn
> Of my shoulder and quickly, too quickly, I am gone.
>
> (C.P. 497)

The angel, is it real, or an illusion?

> But was it Ulysses? Or was it only the warmth of the sun
> On her pillow? The thought kept beating in her like
>   her heart.
> The two kept beating together. It was only day.
> It was Ulysses and it was not. (C.P. 521)

The sun (phenomena) and its imaginative dress, the ordering we weave for it, that is all there is in the universe. The world is empty and full, void and plenum:

> It is empty. But a woman in threadless gold
> Burns us with brushings of her dress
>
> And a dissociated abundance of being, (C.P. 445)

The plenum, the summertime of the imagination, is but the sunsparkle in the void; "every thread of summer is at last unwoven" (C.P. 456) and without the weaving of the imagination, when the interior paramour is gone, man is quite alone:

> So summer comes in the end to these few stains
> And the rust and rot of the door through which she went.
>
> The house is empty. But here is where she sat
> To comb her dewy hair, a touchless light,
>
> Perplexed by its darker iridescences.
> This was the glass in which she used to look

At the moment's being, without history,
The self of summer perfectly perceived,

And feel its country gayety and smile
And be surprised and tremble, hand and lip.

This is the chair from which she gathered up
Her dress, the carefulest, commodious weave

Inwoven by a weaver to twelve bells. . . .
The dress is lying, cast-off on the floor.

Now, the first tutoyers of tragedy
Speak softly, to begin with, in the eaves. (C.P. 428)[23]

The discarded dress was simply one more of the

Generations of the imagination piled
In the manner of its stitchings, of its thread,
In the weaving round the wonder of its need. (C.P. 434)

§ 41   Everybody (almost everybody) in the poems wears clothes; it is not so obvious to the uninitiated reader of Stevens that everybody wears "hats" also (see § 3). The sort of hat a person wears suggests his approach, his style, towards life. Each man has his own unique circumstances, sensibilities, environment, and the man-as-poet will "tip" or "top" or "cap" his view of reality by the slight twist or twirl of his "hat." The hat is another figure for an order imposed upon chaotic reality, and, again, some hats are better than others.

23. The fiction is woven at midnight, "Twelve bells." The poem is about the loss of a "moment" of equilibrium. "Country gayety" is the feeling in the presence of "local objects." The hand and lip (gesture and speech) tremble in the attempt to project the feelings into words.

Though the hat is meant, in part, to keep the burning sun from one's eyes, it should not be such as to keep out light completely:

> The walker in the moonlight walked alone,
> And in his heart his disbelief lay cold.
> His broad-brimmed hat came close upon his eyes. (C.P. 77)

Rosenbloom's bearers wear turbans (C.P. 80), obviously the wrong sort of headpiece, though just why it is harder to say. They are treading where they cannot (in the sky) and, to Stevens' mind, believing what they should not; they are maudlin and absurd to Stevens, and perhaps all this is enough to account for a bizzare chapeau. The revolutionists (C.P. 102) wear a "helmet without reason," since, to Stevens, intense patriotism to the real, to the capitan geloso, is as foolish as belief in various myths (against which the revolt took place); a sort of serious clowning is the only honest posture for the revolutionists with no platform (see § 12). The rationalists, the "meta-men," "cold with an impotency that they know," wear "hats of angular flick and fleck." (C.P. 449)[24]

All objects exterior to the self need to be "a little changed by the tips of artifice" (C.P. 350) so as to fit into some order that establishes a relation of man with the exterior world. The "tipping," the "curving," the imaginative distorting that the poet makes to order reality discloses his essential humanity, his unconcealed desire for the fictive covering:

> The importance of its hat to a form becomes
> More definite. The sweeping brim of the hat
> Makes of the form Most Merciful Capitan

24. For "angular," see § 11.

> The flare
> In the sweeping brim becomes the origin
> Of a human evocation. (C.P. 379)

So cold is the exterior world of things to human desire, so necessary to the endurance of life is imaginative myth-making, that the myth (the hat) makes us what we are, composes a self for the individual, and, if effective enough, for a nation:

> . . . men make themselves their speech: the hard hidalgo
> Lives in the mountainous character of his speech;
>
> And in that mountainous mirror Spain acquires
> The knowledge of Spain and of the hidalgo's hat—
>
> A seeming of the Spaniard, a style of life,
> The invention of a nation in a phrase. (C.P. 345)

§ 42   The poet, finally, goes beyond this composing of the self to the disciplined meditation upon all the compositions of the self that have been or could be made, upon the bulk of poetry made thus far and the potential poetry of the future. The products of the human imagination are, for Stevens, the only comprehensible divinity, man's true object of worship. The myth-making capacity in man gives life its fictive values, and hence is some sort of god-head. The figure of the "Major Man" represents, simply, the sum total of man's plausible projections of himself. Now, to set up as a figure of god a cumulative body of myth is, it would appear, at once a most audacious and a most pathetic attempt at ordering reality. It is the response of a "sensibility in desperation." But it is the prevalent answer of our age; it is the answer which so sickened Jonathan Swift, but it is an honest answer. The figure of the Major Man is, in one sense, a shameful "evading metaphor." Stevens' projection can give the reader, momentarily, all the comfort of a paternalistic deity. It is the comfort of rhetoric, to be sure, but, on the other hand, it is Stevens' very point that the comforts of rhetoric are just as real, while being just as illusory, as the comforts of any other fiction in which the mind chooses to believe.

"The sum total of man's plausible projections of himself." The definition is a blanket one, and needs further elaboration. Each imaginative man makes a different selection of projections; one's "Major Man" is different from everyone else's. And, of course, his own total of projections changes, is added to and subtracted from; one never looks at the same god-head twice. What is a *plausible* projection of oneself? Stevens dances gingerly around this question at all times. The fiction must be true to reality, but it must distort reality—it must be a mixture of fact and fiction. This is saying very little. We are speaking about a process which admits of degrees as if it were one of absolutes. Stevens realizes all this, and one can feel in the following passage the irony towards his "collective being":

> Last night at the end of night his starry head,
> Like the head of fate, looked out in darkness, part
> Thereof and part desire and part the sense
> Of what men are. The collective being knew
> There were others like him safely under roof. (C.P. 299)[25]

The poems of the "hero" can never exhaust man's spirit, or his desire for fictions:

25. "Part" is a word which Stevens flourishes whenever he wishes to convey beneath his rhetoric the fact that he has no other unifying concept, no order to offer man.

I sing a hero's head, large eye
And bearded bronze, but not a man,

Although I patch him as I can
And reach through him almost to man. (C.P. 165)[26]

The poems of the hero can never deal with reality alone:

. . . They are characters beyond
Reality, composed thereof. They are
The fictive man created out of men.
They are men but artificial men. (C.P. 335)

The imagination fuses the real self with the desire for a
fuller being to create a projection of the self which is larger
than life. A "giant" thus formed may be a false, vicious
giant (with "hacker" see C.P. 6) if the projection was based
on a false formulation of man and of his place in reality.
Or it may be a true giant who, with the greater strength of
the imagination, fights against the "murderous alphabet" of
chaos (C.P. 179). And generally, Stevens, with his characteristic double vision, sees his Major Men, his projections of
the self, as necessary though unreal, of noble height though
soon to be deflated:

Now, I, Chocorua, speak of this shadow as
A human thing. It is an eminence,
But of nothing, trash of sleep that will disappear
With the special things of night, little by little,
In day's constellation, and yet remain, yet be,

Not father, but bare brother, megalfrere,

26. The concept of "parts" is carried to its grotesque conclusion in
    the various dismemberments of Stevens' fictive deity, cf. "Star-
    vation's head" (C.P. 254), "Cuisine Bourgeoise" (C.P. 227), "A
    Primitive Like an Orb" (C.P. 443)

Or by whatever boorish name a man
Might call the common self, interior fons. (C.P. 300–1)[27]

The figure of Major Man was a slow-developing one in
Stevens' mind. There are giants in *Harmonium,* but any
serious attempt to formulate in quasi-religious terms a belief
in the past and future of poetry would not have suited the
urbane dandy of that first volume.[28] There is a hint of Major
Man in what Stevens says of himself in the thirties:

Men and the affairs of men seldom concerned
This pundit of the weather, who never ceased
To think of man the abstraction, the comic sum. (C.P. 156)

It was logical then for a man of this temper of mind, when
exalting the imaginative faculty, to come to use as a binding
figure in his system this composite man who summed up the
imaginative achievements of all men as well as their comic
futilities. But the destructive, ironic or comic impulse is very
strong in Stevens, and in "Owl's Clover" (1936), he cannot
give himself up to being an unswerving disciple to the
imagination:

It may be the future depends on an orator,
Some pebble-chewer practiced in Tyrian speech,
An apparition, twanging instruments
Within us hitherto unknown, he that
Confounds all opposites and spins a sphere

27. Chocorua, an actual mountain, is here a personification of the
    "Rock" (see § 25).
28. Daniel Fuchs, in a very fine book on Stevens (see "Bibliog-
    raphy"), treats of Stevens' dandyism and its antecedents in his
    first chapter. (He, too, finds in Stevens, that "sartorial elegance
    hides disarray," and notes the "panic and tension in Stevens'
    affirmations").

Created, like a bubble, of bright sheens,
With a tendency to bulge as it floats away. (O.P. 63)[29]

One trouble is that if the poet is to preach the imagination
as the ultimate value for the future, he must consider as part
of the "sum" the Major Man of the socialist mob:

> . . . conceive what these hands from Sweden mean,
> These English noses and edged, Italian eyes,
> Massed for a head they mean to make for themselves,
> From which their grizzled voice will speak and be heard.
>
> (O.P. 60)

The poet must consider whether anyone can ever give form
to the "sprawling portent," the dark vision of modern man
and modern society:

> The form
> Of a generation that does not know itself,
> Still questioning if to crush the soaring stacks,
> The churches, . . .
> And the people suddenly evil, waked, accused,
> Destroyed by a vengeful movement of the arms,
> A mass overtaken by the blackest sky. (O.P. 68–69)

The poet who believes that the only order is an aesthetic
order is faced with the utter, intense subjectivity of that
order. Such a poet feels that he can impose no order on the
world, on everybody else; he can only bring some semblance
of order to himself. The poet, alienated from belief in any
given myth, is a special person, a custodian of the imagination, living in a cold "cell." He has no real responsibility
to society (though he serves a function in it). The poet is one
of those numerous minor "heroes" whose crystal hymns,

29. For "Tyrian" see "purple" § 14. For "apparition," see "ghost"
    § 10. For "sphere" see "orb" § 12.

fused out of the Rock and the Self, reverberate for each other. These hymns are heroic acts, and their creation promotes a feeling of awe in the poet for the heroic capacities of man's imagination:

> A thousand crystals' chiming voices,
> Like the shiddow-shaddow of lights revolving
> To momentary ones, are blended,
> In hymns, through iridescent changes,
> Of the apprehending of the hero.
> These hymns are like a stubborn brightness
> Approaching in the dark approaches
> Of time and place, becoming certain,
> The organic centre of responses,
> Naked of hindrance, a thousand crystals.   (C.P. 279–80)

> It is not an image. It is a feeling.
> There is no image of the hero.
> There is a feeling as definition
> How could there be an image, an outline,
> A design, a marble soiled by pigeons?
> The hero is a feeling.[30]

> We have and are the man, capable
> Of his brave quickenings, the human
> Accelerations that seem inhuman.

> Say that the hero is his nation,
> In him made one, and in that saying
> Destroy all references.   (C.P. 278–9)

The "hero' 'is then both the Imagination and its achievements; "he" is any interior order of the self which fights against the exterior disorder:

30. Images ordered in poems, or "sculpture," are not true representation of the feelings of the moment (see § 68).

Out of the hero's being, the deliverer

Delivering the prisoner by his words,
So that the skeleton in the moonlight sings,
Sings of an heroic world beyond the cell,

No, not believing, but to make the cell
A hero's world in which he is the hero.
Man must become the hero of his world. (C.P. 261)[31]

The visions of the patriarchs were really hallucinations of
desire for such an order in the exterior world:

The point of vision and desire are the same.
It is to the hero of midnight that we pray
On a hill of stones to make beau mont thereof.
                                        (C.P. 466)[32]

Stevens is ever caught up in a double perspective, in debate
with himself as disciple or skeptic. One side of his mind is
the mocking "hautboy," laughing at the inner hero; the
other is at one with the philosophers who find that man's
imaginings, both past and to come (Major Man), make him
close enough to god-like:

If you say on the hautboy man is not enough,
Can never stand as god, is ever wrong
In the end, however naked, tall, there is still
The impossible possible philosophers' man
The man who has had the time to think enough,
The central man, the human globe, responsive

31. For "cell," see "walls" § 7.
32. There are overtones in this passage, as elsewhere, of the hero
as Christ (on Calvary). The "hero of midnight" is Major Man.

> As a mirror with a voice, the man of glass,
> Who in a million diamonds sums us up. (C.P. 250)[33]

"Gigantomachia" (C.P. 289) presents the poet or hero as "soldier" fighting "giants" (bad giants), striving

> To strip off the complacent trifles,
> To expel the ever-present seductions,
> To reject the script for its lack-tragic,
> To confront with plainest eye the changes. (C.P. 289)

The "giants" of the past were romantic myths that followed such an unacceptable script. In rejecting this script (an old "giant") and looking within for a new one "each man himself became a giant tipped out with largeness" (C.P. 289). The same battle against bad giants is taking place, in a comic frame, in "Bantams in Pine Woods" (C.P. 75). There is a ten-foot fowl, abnormal, perverse. It is a cock that deals in universals, If-you-can of As-can. Any myth not impossible to disprove is food for As-can. He is a transcendentalist who believes the sun is "blackamoor" to bear his blazing tail. The less pretentious poet, the inchling, warns that no one can encompass the universe. Each bantam has only phenomenological knowledge. Each can tip the pines (local objects) around himself by the shaping faculty of the imagination, but the "hoos" of universals are out.

"Jumbo" is another overinflated giant, a transcendentalist who sees only man in the universe, and man in a central position in it:

> Loud, general, large, fat, soft
> And wild and free, the secondary man,

---

33. For "Mirror" and "glass" as figures of the mind, see § 7. See also the discussion of Major Man as the "Supreme Fiction" (rather than "Supreme Being") in Chapter 11.

Ancestor of Narcissus, prince
Of the secondary men. There are no rocks
And stones, only this imager. (C.P. 269)

But the battle for an acceptable mythology does not go on simply between jumbos and heroes. A giant or a Major Man can suffice for an age, or perhaps, just for a mood, a summer's day and then have to be done away with. Time was when the fear of thunder provoked simple country people to produce god-myths. We are more sophisticated today, and, face to face with the void, the business of giant-killing, killing yesterday's good giant, has become a constantly necessary, very pathetic occupation:

Millions of major men against their like
Make more than thunder's rural rumbling. They make
The giants that each one of them becomes
In a calculated chaos. (C.P. 307)

The killing is "calculated" because the poet has come to realize that only by a constant re-invigoration of the spirit through fresh imaginings can he endure. Reality itself is a terrible, inexplicable giant,

Part of the question that is a giant himself:
Of what is this house composed if not of the sun,
These houses, these difficult objects, dilapidate
Appearances of what appearances? (C.P. 465)

The only answer Stevens can give to this impossible question about the dark giant of reality (the multiplicity of things) is to destroy him by another, more tolerable giant, a giant of the imagination:

Dark things without a double, after all,
Unless a second giant kills the first—
A recent imagining of reality. (C.P. 465)

This is the final vision of Stevens concerning all this myth-making. Out of an inscrutable world, a nothingness for man, the poet has brought forth, and will ever bring forth hairs, birds, foyers, palms, cloaks, giants, what image you will, figures, myths, letters, that come and go, sustain and disgust, all flowing simply from a compulsion for order that lies deep beneath the rational life:

> That's it. The lover writes, the believer hears,
> The poet mumbles and the painter sees,
> Each one, his fated eccentricity,
> As a part, but part, but tenacious particle,
> Of the skeleton of the ether, the total
> Of letters, prophecies, perceptions, clods
> Of color, the giant of nothingness, each one
> And the giant ever changing, living in change.   (C.P. 443)

Chapter Five

Figures of Change

What hast thou, O my soul, with paradise?
Will we not rather, when our freedom's won,
Get us to some clear place wherein the sun
Lets drift in on us through the olive leaves
A liquid glory? If at Sirmio,
My soul, I meet thee, when this life's outrun,
Will we not find some headland consecrated
By aery apostles of terrene delight,
Will not our cult be founded on the waves,
Clear sapphire, cobalt, cyanine,
On triune azures, the impalpable
Mirrors unstill of the eternal change?
                    Ezra Pound, "Blandula, Tenulla, Vagula"

The west wind was the music, the motion, the force
To which the swans curveted, a will to change,
A will to make iris frettings on the blank. (C.P. 397)

§ 43   "Death is the mother of beauty," Stevens asserts
rather ironically in "Sunday Morning," "hence from her,
alone, shall come fulfillment to our dreams and our desires."
Ironic, that is, because the "fulfillment" is the annihilation of
our dreams and our desires. We will never be fulfilled, but we
can feel beauty in moments more acutely because of the
pressures of time and annihilation. And if these moments

are all we have, then "life is motion"; the measure of life is the ability to keep moving into new moments of equilibrium. The world is moving, the wind and air and clouds. We are moving, towards death every year, into new environments of sun and sea and mood every day, every moment. The imagination must play with all the inconstants, bend them to its purpose. It must turn the wind to music, the air to speech, clouds to crystal, formlessness into fictive form:

> It was as if thunder took form upon
> The piano, that time; the time when the crude
> And jealous grandeurs of sun and sky
> Scattered themselves in the garden, like
> The wind dissolving into birds,
> The clouds becoming braided girls.
> It was like the sea poured out again
> In east wind beating the shutters at night.[1]
>
> The crude and jealous formlessness
> Became the form and the fragrance of things
> Without clairvoyance.   (C.P. 246–7)

The process is nevertheless one of making "iris frettings on the blank," or turning the eternal west wind eastward. The figures Stevens uses to represent the eternal change are archetypal ones, including, besides those we have touched on, the Wheel and the Fire. But, characteristically, these figures in Stevens often have "two sides" which give them an originality in context. There is little point in dwelling on these figures when their significations are quite accessible. The attempt here will be only to establish Stevens' mixed emotions towards these familiar figures of change.[2]

Life is motion (C.P. 83), a constant marrying of "flesh and

1. For "garden," see "park," § 31, and Susanna's garden § 55. For "birds" § 39. "Braids" § 26. "East" § 15.
2. Of course, in a sense, all of Stevens' figures are figures of change,

air," of human desire with the blank, performed by the imagination. One connects with one's environment, one's "weather," in a dubious relationship. It is not always possible to do even this:

> It comes about that the drifting of these curtains
> Is full of long motions; as the ponderous
> Deflations of distance; or as clouds
> Inseparable from their afternoons;
> Or the changing of light, the dropping
> Of the silence, wide sleep and solitude
> Of night, in which all motion
> Is beyond us, as the firmament,
> Up-rising and down-falling, bares
> The last largeness, bold to see. (C.P. 62)[3]

Only some motions in the universe are manageable. The fictive "covering" of the imagination (the "curtains") can shape a not-too-violent motion by "deflating" (the choice of word is deliberate, of course) the long distance of the wind's sweep. Then, in an equilibrium of flesh (the poet's desire) and air (nothingness), "clouds are inseparable from their afternoons," and the world as it has been caught for a moment is sufficient for the spirit. Finally, the imagination can no longer hold the vast and impersonal motions of the universe in check, and this is the death of the moment.

The sun (ever shifting, changing, moving light) can mingle too with imaginative phantasy to create new "bodies"

since their effectiveness does not last, and a return to un-abstracted reality, without evading metaphor, is always part of the process. The eye ("iris") makes "frets" on the blank reality.
3. The tantalizing curtains are in the "house" (the mind) of a metaphysician, but he is a poet, too, as all philosophers are, looking with awe at the unmanageable universe. The curtains, in part, represent the veils of sense perception for the meta-physician. For the poet they represent the "draping" of reality.

to comfort us. But they are deceptions, as the deception of catching of the wind in the curtains:

> The body walks forth naked in the sun
> And, out of tenderness or grief, the sun
> Gives comfort, so that other bodies come,
> Twinning our phantasy and our device,
> And apt in versatile motion, touch and sound
> To make the body covetous in desire
> Of the still finer, more implacable chords.
> So be it. Yet the spaciousness and light
> In which the body walks and is deceived,
> Falls from that fatal and that barer sky,
> And this the spirit sees and is aggrieved. (C.P. 108)

For the greatest deception is to feel that the sun, the phenomenological universe, holds any tenderness or grief. It is the body's desire that impels the whole phantasy.

Man has to go through all sorts of spiritual contortions to live under a fatal sky:

> . . . the acrobat observed
> The universal machine. There he perceived
> The need for a thesis, a music constant to move.
>
> (O.P. 82)

"Music" must move because the human desire for order and for permanence takes different forms in different ages, in different moments:

> The truth is that there comes a time
> When we can mourn no more over music
> That is so much motionless sound.
> There comes a time when the waltz
> Is no longer a mode of desire, a mode
> Of revealing desire and is empty of shadows.
>
> Too many waltzes have ended. (C.P. 121)

Especially in our age, the search for "sound free from motion" (see C.P. 268) is absurd. We must make music from the "hurricane," the "storm" of reality. Now our music hardly outlasts the making:

> I know my lazy, leaden twang
> Is like the reason in a storm;
>
> And yet it brings the storm to bear.
> I twang it out and leave it there. (C.P. 169)

Finally, in our modern "epic of disbelief" motion alone, a moving from poem to poem, the "pleasures of merely circulating" (C.P. 149), keep the poet from the void. The music becomes:

> A thing final in itself and, therefore, good:
> One of the vast repetitions final in
> Themselves and, therefore, good, the going round
>
> And round and round, the merely going round
> Until merely going round is a final good. (C.P. 405)

In a late poem of Stevens there is a splendid evocation of the power of natural motion and violent change to stimulate to the imaginative moment (to "music") the aging poet, a man under the portent of the "westward" evening star:

> There was a crush of strength in a grinding going round,
> Under the front of the westward evening star,
>
> The vigor of glory, a glittering in the veins,
> As things emerged and moved and were dissolved,
>
> Either in distance, change or nothingness,
> The visible transformations of summer night,

> An argentine abstraction approaching form
> And suddenly denying itself away. (O.P. 110)

But the "moments" come rarely. In time, and inevitably with age, the integration of flesh and air dissipates, and the caress is again just a motion:

> She gives transparence. But she has grown old. . . .
> The soft hands are a motion not a touch. (C.P. 413)

§ 44   The wind in Stevens partakes of two opposing significations that are quite clear. On the one hand, the wind is a destructive force, one necessary to cathartic change:

> A tempest cracked on the theatre. Quickly,
> The wind beat in the roof and half the walls. (C.P. 306)

On the other hand, the wind is, in itself, a beneficent afflatus, carrying the imagination's fiction over the sea of chaos:

> The wind speeds her,
> Blowing upon her hands
> And watery back.
> She touches the clouds, where she goes
> In the circle of her traverse of the sea. (C.P. 5)

The imagination is always overcome by the "weather," but, in its "moments," it can bend the winds to its purpose:

> Yet there was a man within me
> Could have risen to the clouds,
> Could have touched these winds,
> Bent and broken them down,
> Could have stood up sharply in the sky. (C.P. 212)

In that final aesthetic vision where desire is completely fulfilled, described in "Of Mere Being" (see § 34), the wind

moves *slowly* through the branches of the palm at the edge
of space. Motion there is perfectly controlled and in equilibrium with everything else. The soft life-giving motion is
never-ending, and so is the song and the life of the gold-
feathered bird. The birds' "firefangled feathers dangle down"
(see § 34). Continual flight or motion is no longer necessary;
the bird can settle in repose, and yet not fall into the "ocean,
the geography of the dead" (C.P. 304).

§ 45   This is the vision of desire fulfilled, the wind controlled, the ocean disdained. But it is an impossible vision.
The "wind" is not the worse we have to face. It is the
"ocean," the overwhelming multiplicity of things, that is
really uncontrollable:

>   . . . Hans heard,
> By his drift-fire, on the shore, the difference
> Between loud water and loud wind, between that
> Which has no accurate syllables and that
> Which cries *so blau* and cries again *so lind*
> Und *so lau,* between sound without meaning and speech.
>   (C.P. 421)

Everything that Stevens has to say about the sea is in that
quintessential poem of his, "The Idea of Order at Key West."

> She sang beyond the genius of the sea.
> The water never formed to mind or voice,
>
>   . . . and yet its mimic motion
> Made constant cry, caused constantly a cry,
> That was not ours although we understood,
> Inhuman, of the veritable ocean.   (C.P. 128)

The cry of the *veritable* ocean is inhuman and cannot be

controlled. The Imagination ("she"), by disdaining the sea cry can create her own mundo in which to live for a time.[4]

§ 46   The ocean represents the whole of chaos, and for the whole we have no ordering principle, only for "parts." There is a "dumbfoundering abyss" between the "ocean" and our subjective desires that only poetry, "good speech," "good air" can attempt to bridge, at least for one's own self:

> Good air, good friend, what is there in life?
>
> Is it ideas that I believe?
> Good air, my only friend, believe,
>
> Believe would be a brother full
> Of love, believe would be a friend,
> Friendlier than my only friend,
> Good air.   (C.P. 175–6)

But this is air seen subjectively; an objective look clears the air of friendly phantoms:

> Today the air is clear of everything.
> It has no knowledge except of nothingness
> And it flows over us without meanings.   (O.P. 113)

Air is what we breathe, it merely sustains the body. From within, alone, comes the forming of the meaningless air into meaningful speech, meaningful, this is, to ourselves:

> Air is air,
> Its vacancy glitters round us everywhere.
> Its sounds are not angelic syllables

4. On the surface of the poem, this mundo is projected as unending—as indeed it is if the life of the cumulative achievements of the human imagination is seen as the life of the world. But for any particular poet, the mundo suffices momentarily and then not at all.

But our unfashioned spirits realized
More sharply in more furious selves.   (C.P. 137)

The poet, in old age, relaxes the tensions of integration,
the attempts to link by the imagination the objective real
and subjective human desires, and accepts, finally, the trans-
parent air, formlessness, motion, change, and mere color for
what they are. The younger poet cannot, and should not, do
so; it is even a little frightening for the old poet who has so
little left to lose:

No doubt we live beyond ourselves in air,

In an element that does not do for us,
So well, that which we do for ourselves, too big,
A thing not planned for imagery or belief,

Not one of the masculine myths we used to make,
A transparency through which the swallow weaves,
Without any form or any sense of form,

What we know in what we see, what we feel in what
We hear, what we are, beyond mystic disputation,
In the tumult of integrations out of the sky,

And what we think, a breathing like the wind,
A moving part of a motion, a discovery
Part of a discovery, a change part of a change,

A sharing of color and being part of it.   (C.P. 518)

§ 47   What we see, what we feel, and what we think shift
and change. "Clouds" can figure this moving, shifting, and
changing of our "cloudy" perceptions of reality. The tumults
of the winds, the sea, the refractions of the sun's rays, the

iridescence in the air, can give variable coloring, motion, and shape to clouds in the sky, and these changes of appearances in clouds can serve poetically to suggest subtle fluctuations in emotion, changes in mood and changes in ideas, in what we think. "Sea Surface Full of Clouds" is a tour de force in projecting some of these fluctuating perceptions, emotions and ideas, and in representing their integrations and dissipations. It begins:

> In that November off Tehuantepec,
> The slopping of the sea grew still one night
> And in the morning summer hued the deck
>
> And made one think of rosy chocolate
> And gilt umbrellas. Paradisal green
> Gave suavity to the perplexed machine
>
> Of ocean, which like limpid water lay.
> Who, then, in that ambrosial latitude
> Out of the light evolved the moving blooms,
>
> Who, then, evolved the sea-blooms from the clouds
> Diffusing balm in that Pacific calm?
> *C'était mon enfant, mon bijou, mon âme.*
>
> The sea-clouds whitened far below the calm
> And moved, as blooms move, in the swimming green
> And in its watery radiance, while the hue
>
> Of heaven in an antique reflection rolled
> Round those flotillas. And sometimes the sea
> Poured brilliant iris on the glistening blue.   (C.P. 98–9)

The time is November, presumably, in order to suggest that the imagination has its own seasons, can make summer out of late autumn. "Tehuantepec" sounds as though it would provide the gaudy panoramas the poem deals with. The imagination calms the sea, a feat which, it is asserted with finality in the "Idea of Order at Key West," is impossible, except in that green mundo of the imagination. In this particular mundo one thinks of rosy (dawn-color?) chocolate (a confection) and gilt (by the sun's color?) umbrellas (parasols). It is the imagination, Stevens' "âme," which evolves tinted blooms from light and cloud. Below the calm, the ordered surface of ocean (where the clouds have color), the true "whiteness" of cloud is apparent. The sea blooms evolved from cloud are moving, changing, dissipating. The "blue' 'of sea and sky tint the cloud, a blue that will serve for a while and then turn white. This particular integration, figured as a sea bloom, comes and goes; fresh integrations of new moods and perceptions will follow, to be dissipated in their turn, all "impalpable/Mirrors unstill of the eternal change." The process goes on and on. The poem ends:

> The sovereign clouds came clustering. The conch
> Of loyal conjuration trumped. The wind
> Of green blooms turning crisped the motley hue.
>
> To clearing opalescence. Then the sea
> And heaven rolled as one and from the two
> Came fresh transfigurings of freshest blue. (C.P. 102)

The sky and sea roll "as" one, but they *are* two. The transfiguring integration is fictional. The clouds are "sovereign" in that they are real. The Imagination conjures colors till the wind clears the spell. The poem is masterful in its maintenance of a double attitude towards the "transfigurings." One feels implicit in every line emotions both of awe and of irony concerning what the imagination can do (as in "rosy chocolates and gilt umbrellas").

Clouds emphatically do not contain revelations:

> . . . these lights [imaginative insights] are not a spell
> of light,
> A saying out of a cloud, but innocence.
> An innocence of the earth and no false sign
>
> Or symbol of malice. That we partake thereof,
> Lie down like children in this holiness. (C.P. 418)

Children we are, with no fathers, "benevolences, distant heads" (C.P. 317), in the clouds. The universe is enwrapped in cloud; we cannot pierce the "physical fix of things." Yet there is a deeply felt human desire to do so, to understand the "unfamiliar, difficult fern, pushing and pushing red after red" (C.P. 365). We cannot get at the core of existence, we are limited to our sense perception, always at a cloudy second remove from objects, beyond relation to the center:

> There are doubles of this fern in clouds,
> Less firm than the paternal flame,
> Yet drenched with its identity,
> Reflections and off-shoots, mimic-motes
>
> And mist-mites, dangling seconds, grown
> Beyond relation to the parent trunk:
> The dazzling, bulging, brightest core,
> The furiously burning father-fire. . . . (C.P. 365)

The Paltry Nude, bare bones of a fiction, "touches the clouds" (C.P. 5); this is the extreme height the imagination can project. All the poet can do is accept the "drifting waste" of sun and cloud and magnify the little he has in his imaginative fictions. The address below is to the clouds and about the imagination's magnifying of them:

So speech of your processionals returns
In the casual evocations of your tread
Across the stale, mysterious seasons. These
Are the music of meet resignation; these
The responsive, still sustaining pomps for you
To magnify, if in that drifting waste
You are to be accompanied by more
Than mute bare splendors of the sun and moon. (C.P. 56)

The "costuming of clouds" (C.P. 139) is all we have and the
poet makes the best of it. "Herr Doktor" the metaphysician
omits "reefs of clouds" (perceptions which do not relate to
an order) from his thinking (see C.P. 162). Konstantinov, the
logician in 'Esthetique du Mal' is not "aware of the clouds,
lighting the martyrs of logic with white fire" (C.P. 325).

But still a poetry of the natural world cannot satisfy
human desire completely:

I know that I cannot be mended,
Out of the clouds, pomp of the air,
By which at least I am befriended. (C.P. 201)

This is decidedly a one-way friendship. The cycles of the
weather go on, of course, regardless of whether a perceiver
is around:

Death is absolute and without memorial
As in a season of autumn,
When the wind stops,

When the wind stops and, over the heavens,
The clouds go, nevertheless,
In their direction. (C.P. 97)

§ 48   At times the Imagination can make one satisfied to
simply move along with nature, on the "wheel" of flux:

It is least what one ever sees.
It is only the way one feels, to say
Where my spirit is I am,
To say the light wind worries the sail,
To say the water is swift today,

To expunge all people and be a pupil
Of the gorgeous wheel   (C.P. 120–1)

The gorgeous wheel is gorgeous only sometimes. Nature is inhuman, "the wheel survives the myths" (C.P. 222). And, like the circle (§ 13), "the merely revolving wheel returns and returns, along the dry, salt shore" (O.P. 81). The image is of the endless rise and fall of the waves of ocean on the dry salt shore of reality.

Over and over, the weather changes, and we are free to make of it what we will. But to fix the weather, to stop the wheel, to attempt to escape the fire and flux of life, is the folly of human desire. The wind, the snow, the clouds, the air, are, like everything else, "fidgets of all-related fire" (see C.P. 352). This real fire, which is the father-fire, is incommensurable with human wants, but a lesser fire, the candle of the imagination, can create for us, momentarily, a mundo that satisfies the deep desire for permanence, can give us Sirmio for paradise:

. . . the candle tearing against the wick
To join a hovering excellence, to escape
From fire and be part only of that of which

Fire is the symbol: the celestial possible. (C.P. 509)

PART TWO

Structural Figuration

Chapter Six

Double Vision in Whole Poems

Unreal, give back to us what once you gave
The imagination that we spurned and crave.
      "To The One Of Fictive Music" (C.P. 88)

§ 49   We have looked so far at the "disparate halves" of specific figures, and pointed out the tensions that Stevens' double attitude toward a figure produces in local passages throughout the poems, wherever the figure may occur. Stevens' double vision of what he is doing, his mixed feelings concerning the value of the imaginative act, is, of course, often figured (using "figuration" in the broad sense), in the design of whole poems. For instance, a person may utter doctrinal truths which his situation or his posture render ironic or, at best, half truth. A statement in a last stanza may undercut, or modify, or even reverse a statement in the first, whenever honesty to human desire demands a tempering of doctrinal zeal. Or, frequently, concurrent with rousing doctrinal avowals will flow cries, uttered compulsively, of skepticism, and of little doctrinal faith. And so the poems exhibit their odd, troubled surfaces which have led many critics either to damn them for willful obscurity, or to see them from one side only, glozing over sections that undercut the line they are prepounding. The attempt now will be to establish, using the results of the examinations of specific figures

125

above, the complexity of attitudes and emotions that lie beneath a number of Stevens' finest poems.

We noticed before, in our introduction, that the true subject of poetry for Stevens is the real object; the poetry of the subject is the imaginative distortion of the object. It is inevitable in a poet who views what he is doing in these severe terms that he will fluctuate between a need to spurn and a need to crave the fictive mundo, between moods of disgust and moods of desire. A given Stevens poem has a dominant key of one mood, but usually the other is also, to some extent, there. "Belshazzar" in "Country Words" (C.P. 207), for instance, embodies the two attitudes at the same time.[1] He is, first, a figure for an outworn myth where people used to see other people as the Lord's representatives: "putrid rock pillar of a putrid people." But where do the myths of Belshazzars come from? They flow from the people's desire to make diamonds out of the rock of reality. The poet sings in a *canton* (district) of Belshazzar, now the "rock." The sun in imaginative moments might appear and "redden" "great Belshazzar's brow" (see § 25). From the rock, the true Belshazzar, the true subject, comes a mythic false Belshazzar, the poetry of the subject. Fictive Belshazzars come, decay, and go, brought up by the poet's desire to make diamond from rock by making "words" of "local objects," "country things."

> What is it that my feeling seeks?
> I know from all the things it touched

1. I will assume here and in all the analyses to follow that the reader has *Collected Poems* before him, and so is in no need of extensive quotation. Each poem should be read carefully before these rather compressed analyses are examined, if only to test whether one's own impressions of the tonality of a given poem run counter to mine.

And left beside and left behind.
It wants the diamond pivot bright.
It wants Belshazzar reading right
The luminous pages on his knee, (C.P. 207)

"Pages on his knee" refers to objects "at the foot" of Belshazzar, the mountain, the real (pages that the "large red man" reads). The poet's song is rebellious because the old Belshazzar myth is putrid; any myth grows putrid. Will the poet's feeling ever find the "diamond pivot" that it seeks? Only "if the cloud that hangs upon the heart and round the mind cleared from the north." From what we know already of Stevens, there are "moments" when the "cloud" (see § 47) will seem to rise from the heart, from human desire, but it will never clear from round the mind (see § 7). This is another of the hundreds of "if" answers in Stevens that merely straddle a double, ambiguous attitude. The outer edges of the song are always fuzzy because the song never fulfils desire; all mundos are "left beside and left behind." The song is "cunningly" constructed to express both the disgust with putrid fictions and the desire for a new fiction that will, alas, begin to putrefy at the moment of birth. One is uneasy reading this poem precisely because he can sense that the poetic mind behind it is expressing an uneasiness.

§ 50   "Homunculus et la Belle Etoile" (C.P. 25), by the preciousness of its title, prepares us for an ironic tone in the poem. Homunculus, the little spirit-man, is a whimsical figure for the human desire for moonlight, for illusion, whether it be in drunkards, poets, widows, or philosophers. They all want to see the actual star (the "true subject") as "la belle étoile," or the "young emerald." Yet this is not a poem of disgust but of desire. The moonlight is illusion, but it makes life beautiful, charming, fecund:

> It is a good light, then, for those
> That know the ultimate Plato,
> Tranquillizing with this jewel
> The torments of confusion. (C.P. 27)

Knowledge of the "ultimate Plato" is to know that beyond the Platonic Forms, which philosophers create to make order out of chaos, is chaos and confusion, but that these forms, these jewels (imaginative mundos) tranquilize the Homunculus within us, and are hence life's ultimate value. Everyone lives an illusion, most of all the philosopher who builds systems out of desire, but one must make emeralds out of stars in order to face the star (as object) at all. The philosopher is much like the poets, who in their "cloaks" pay reverence to their "mistress," the Imagination.

§ 51   But the process is one of *conscious* fabrication, and so it is a sort of tense tranquility we can attain. The "paltry nude" longs for a condition which is equivocal at best, for a time when she

> Will go, like the centre of sea-green pomp,
> In an intenser calm,
> Scullion of fate,
> Across the spick torrent, ceaselessly,
> Upon the irretrievable way. (C.P. 6)

Our modern Venus is seen as a poor scullion who has a menial position and no purpose, since the sea is "spick." There are, that is, no connections between a fiction of the sea-Venus and the real sea save those which we create and find delight in.

§ 52   A poem where disgust concerning the imagination predominates over desire is "The Emperor of Ice Cream." (C.P. 64) One must sense, it seems to me, that the "muscular one" is not engaged in a very noble occupation, or looked on with particular favor by Stevens. Anyone who has read, say, "Loneliness in Jersey City," noted Stevens' attitude to the "mob" there, or who is familiar with the fastidiousness of Stevens everywhere, cannot feel that he is squarely behind the dawdling wenches and the running boys. Nor should one suppose Stevens so vulgar as to be speaking primarily of human death and a human corpse in the lines:

> If her horny feet protrude, they come
> To show how cold she is, and dumb. (C.P. 64)

All these figures are, to be sure, intended to shock, and by shocking our moral sensibilities, to force us to project the poem to the more abstract level of meaning intended, where we see the corpse as a figure for the inhuman universe, so cold to our desire. The corpse, too, can represent the death of myth or transcendant attitudes, in our time. But the corpse and the wake are without embellishment. To Stevens, as the champion of the imagination, this is emphatically *not* the right way to run a funeral; it is without bouquets, without drapery or chant, without imagination.[2] But, in this poem, Stevens is projecting a mood where what the imagination can do to hide the horny feet of reality seems meaningless, a mere whipping up of confections. When he says "Let be be finale of seem" he is asking, not with deep delight, but with a good measure of despair and disgust, whether reality is not better endured without confection, without elaborately evasive metaphor. Do not drape the wenches, make no bowls for the flowers; beautiful imaginative twists are too untrue. Stay with the frivolous distortion, such as the curds, and

2. See Richard Ellmann's "Wallace Stevens' Ice-Cream," *Kenyon Review*, xix (1957), pp. 89–105. The "dresser of deal" and the "sheet with embroidery" represent attitudes of the past.

cream. One must have a dream to cover the corpse (reality), but the emerald or the diamond dreams which temporarily fulfill desire are destroyed so completely when the lamp affixes its beam, when the mind looks squarely at the object, that we, perhaps, should stick to confects of ice-cream, which is more than aspic, though less than manna.

§ 53   The moment of disenchantment is not an easy one for Stevens. His doctrines do not provide palliatives for this sort of time, when the poet, like everybody else, is a "weeping burgher" (see C.P. 61). He says then "It is with a strange malice that I distort the world." But malice towards whom? Is it bad that "ill humors should mask as white girls" etc? Certainly not for the reader. The malice is the pain which the poet inflicts on himself when, inevitably, he is "tortured for old speech," for white, calcined, foppish lines. The plight of the poet as burgher faced by the "sorry verities," the objects of reality, is pathetic, and the only cure is in the excesses of the imagination:

> . . . in excess, continual,
> There is cure of sorrow. (C.P. 61)

Good work if you can keep it up, but we see everywhere in Stevens that this doctrine of constant "circulation" from myth to myth is pure theory, and that there is no way of avoiding sorrow. The fiction vanishes, and the disgust returns:

> . . . how many men have copied dew
> For buttons, how many women have covered themselves
> With dew, dew dresses, stones and chains of dew, heads
> Of the floweriest flowers dewed with the dewiest dew.
> One grows to hate these things except on the dump.
> (C.P. 202)

The man on the dump, like the man who looks at reality as a corpse in "The Emperor of Ice Cream," finds the only "cure" for this temporary disgust in sticking to and "naming" the object alone, "The the." But this is hardly a permanent cure. In a series of poignant questions (never assertions), Stevens indirectly asks himself whether such a cure really suffices.

> Is it a philosopher's honeymoon, one finds
> On the dump? Is it to sit among mattresses of the dead,
> Bottles, pots, shoes and grass and murmur *aptest eve:*
> Is it to hear the blatter of grackles and say
> *Invisible priest;* is it to eject, to pull
> The day to pieces and cry *stanza my stone?*
> Where was it one first heard of the truth? The the.
>
> (C.P. 203)

The absurd position of the man in itself tells us that one cannot live with the object alone. The mind finally demands that images be culled from the dump to give a temporary illusion of permanence and order. The most "well-dressed" man has still his "beard" (improper appendage) of human desire for myth (§ 27), for something firm, infallible, the sweet country of belief, of belief in forms, in angel's aureoles:

> After the final no there comes a yes
> And on that yes the future world depends.
> No was the night. Yes is this present sun.
> If the rejected things, the things denied,
> Slid over the western cataract, yet one,
> One only, one thing that was firm, even
> No greater than a cricket's horn, no more
> Than a thought to be rehearsed all day, a speech
> Of the self that must sustain itself on speech,

One thing remaining, infallible, would be
Enough. Ah! douce campagna of that thing!
Ah! douce campagna, honey in the heart,
Green in the body, out of a petty phrase,
Out of a thing believed, a thing affirmed:
The form on the pillow humming while one sleeps,
The aureole above the humming house . . .

It can never be satisfied, the mind, never.   (C.P. 247)[3]

The mind goes from no to yes, yes to no, constantly, because there is no one thing that is firm, least of all the "petty phrase."

§ 54   But the self must sustain itself on speech. We see three young girls come armed against the giant of reality who bears his hacker (see C.P. 6). One will whisper "heavenly labials [the "petty phrase"] in a world of gutturals," the other will weave the colored draperies of a fiction, another will waft the "civilest odors" out of "unsmelled flowers" of the imagination. It is pathetic, this battle against the giant, pathetic as the "flyer's fall":

This man escaped the dirty fates,
Knowing that he died nobly, as he died.

Darkness, nothingness of human after-death,
Receive and keep him in the deepnesses of space—

Profundum, physical thunder, dimension in which
We believe without belief, beyond belief.   (C.P. 336)

The first stanza has all the glory of old noble poems on the same subject. But for the poet who no longer believes in anything but the physical dimension, in what way does the

---

3.   For "aureole," see § 28. The humming house is the mind (see § 7).

flyer fall nobly? Stevens seems elsewhere to have no senti-
ment about death in war: "the paratroopers fall and as they
fall they mow the lawn" (C.P. 322). The point is, I take it,
that it is the flyer himself who "knows" his death is noble.
For Stevens "knowing" is always really just "feeling." The
flyer felt he was doing the noble thing, and feeling is everything, ("everything is psychic"). And then, too, the flyer, in
one sense, escaped the dirty fates by *dying,* since life finally
would have pushed him to have second thoughts about any
nobility in a flyer's fall.[4]

The poem is a hedge of course. The real tone of the poem
is one of fear and frustration. There is in Stevens always a
hedge beneath the rhetoric:

> Bare night is best. Bare earth is best. Bare, bare,
> Except for our own houses. (C.P. 137–8)

The hedge is necessary if the poet is to keep anything human
in his poems. Honesty to his own fears and to his desires,
however incapable of fulfillment they are, causes the poet
both to spurn and to crave the imagination, to call upon the
unreal, while proclaiming the real, to create compulsively
personæ and situations where the human condition runs
counter to the doctrinal affirmation, to contrast the fate of
the imagination and its fictions with the fate of man.

4. Compare the figure of the "soldier" (§ 9).

Chapter Seven

Peter Quince at the Clavier

§ 55   "Peter Quince" is something like the apotheosis of double vision. Running concurrently throughout the poem (here, perhaps, in more perfect juxtaposition than anywhere else in Stevens) is a fable of the fate of man, and a contrasting description of the processes of the Imagination. The mortality of any given fictive mundo (an imaginative Susanna) is contrasted with the eternity of the imaginative process and the *materia poetica,* the material universe. "Peter Quince" is really a poem about the imaginative faculty, its seasons and its value. It is not a poem about love between the sexes, nor in any way about relations between people. It is, rather, about the poet in solitude carrying on his sometime love affair with his "interior paramour," she who brings forth each "spring" children of desire that of necessity must be raped in "autumn." "Peter Quince' 'is an "amoral" poem in that it does not deal with moral problems at all, but with the inevitable cycles of creation and destruction that is the life of the poetic mind. The skeptical poet has his own obligations to his poems, the "Susannas" he creates, which are antithetical to the obligations that obtain in the love of one person for another.

Susanna figures the imaginative integration or ordering which makes a summer "garden" out of reality, out of the jumble of perceived objects.[1] The grey or black night is temporarily transformed to a "green evening," water is warmed and the winds held in control. The poet, in spring and summer, finds "concealed imaginings" in reality, that is, metaphorical relations between objects that are fictive but delightful, and able for the season to sustain the poet and his desire for order.

Now the red-eyed elders represent that "winter" season of the mind which demands that all metaphorical accretions be stripped from objects of perception while at the same time, is highly desirous of the beauty of an order.[2] The elders are "white" (see § 14) because their spirits are deprived of the imagination's "blue;" their eyes are red because they are focused on red reality (see § 14). They consummate the necessary rape which must be performed upon an outworn fiction, those "spent emotions," "old devotions." The rape is holy, a sanctified ritual carried out after prayer and cowled repentance. Reality's thin blood must be reinvigorated by a new fiction every "spring;" the maiden must die in "winter." 'Hosanna," this religious ritual of the imaginative life, is more important than any given sacrifice, any fictional Susanna:

> The body dies; the body's beauty lives
> So evenings die, in their green going,
> A wave, interminably flowing.
> So gardens die, their meek breath scenting
> The cowl of winter, done repenting.
> So maidens die, to the auroral
> Celebration of a maiden's choral.

1. For the figures of women see § 22. For the figure of the garden see § 31.
2. For this state of mind, see: "The Snow Man," "The Man Whose Pharynx was Bad," "The Man on the Dump," "The Well Dressed Man With a Beard," "Man and Bottle."

Susanna is deflowered and killed, the "evening" and "garden" of her creation go, the cowled elders captured the music, and it has escaped. They retreat to repent their violation, but will emerge in the springtime sweet-scented from their deed. They will presumably rape another Susanna in the next autumn. Another maiden will be sacrificed, while maidens who wait their turn sing a choral song of celebration. Why the celebration, why the religious overtones in the passage? Because the poetic process survives both music and maker.

§ 56   The second section of "Peter Quince" figures the stages in the imaginative process, the integration, dissipation, and destruction of a fiction. A fictional "Susanna" slowly loses its hold on the emotions of its creator in the autumnal season of his creative cycle. Out of the warm water, Susanna is not at first chilled in her nakedness, for she is protected by the "scarves" (§ 40) woven from imaginative desire:

> Upon the bank, she stood
> In the cool
> Of spent emotions.
> She felt, among the leaves,
> The dew
> Of old devotions.
> She walked upon the grass,
> Still quavering.
> The winds were like her maids,
> On timid feet,
> Fetching her woven scarves,
> Yet wavering.

Susanna barely has the winds in control any more (§ 44). In summer, the winds were like her maids, attendant to her, and singing by her side. These "maids" are the "Byzantines" of section three ("Byzantine" carrying suggestions perhaps of "ornateness" and "servility." They figure warm "east" winds turned "westward"). They "whisper" before Susanna's rape, they "simper" after the rape is consummated. The imagination makes music of the wind and rain in summer; in autumn the destructive analytic side of the mind can hear no music in the sound of the wind (see "The Snow Man"). This "mind of winter" which Stevens everywhere considers a necessary phase in the valid imaginative process is figured not only by the elders but also by the "lamp" which shines directly on an object. (The figure recurs in "The Emperor of Ice Cream.")

§ 57   Susanna's music is stilled, but the music did happen, the integration of summer had had its effect on the emotions of the poet and music is, after all, feeling, not sound. Objects in motion, wind and rain, or fingers on keys, may *make* music for our sensibilities, but *are* merely sounds. It is the human desire for order, and the feeling at times that one has it, that is music. The poet in his desire thinks not merely of his mistress (the interior paramour), but of her ornament, her "blue-shadowed silk" (the fabric of the poem woven out of the imagination's "blue"). The interior paramour is the Bullshit "you" addressed here and in other poems, such as "Le Monocle de Mon Oncle" and "To the One of Fictive Music." And one of her fictive songs was of Susanna, who searched the "touch of springs" (a pun on the water in which she lies and on that season of the mind), just as the musician's fingers touch the keys of the clavier, to make music out of one's desires.

Susanna as a figure for the poetic process inevitably loses its effectiveness—beauty is momentary in the mind—but there are other Susannas under other names, and the process of making music is immortal. The impelling force in the process is the human desire to order the vast sea of experience (if only in those rare moments of equilibrium and integration), to find "portals" at the end of thought that will lead us at times to other gardens and warmer water.[3]

Now, the "death" of any given figure for the poetic process is not a very important thing; one loses one's desire to integrate feelings in a certain fashion, and finds another fashion. The "constant sacrament of praise" is for the imagination which produces the music, the integration of feelings. But of course there is another kind of death; the physical Susanna dies, the poet dies, his imagination with him, and of this process no music can be made. Beauty is immortal in the "flesh," but of course not in Susanna's body. "Flesh" (§ 43) figures every man's desire for order (which is a "marriage of flesh and air"). Then too there is here implied the flesh of the world's body, or the material object. "Peter Quince" has dealt in a muted way with these ironies and ambiguities implicit in the contrast between the poetic process and the process of living. The major irony is that physical death finally makes the two processes one, so far as the individual poet is concerned.

Perhaps this is why the poem is entitled "Peter Quince at the Clavier." The Clavier, that refined musical instrument, can serve admirably as a figure for the poetic process; Peter Quince, that fumbling stage manager in *Midsummer Night's Dream,* can perhaps be a figure for the human condition of the poet. Peter Quince's desire to make music of life, to order it, is perhaps as poignant, incongruous and understandable, as the elders' hunger for Susanna.

3.   For "Portals" see § 33.

Chapter Eight

Le Monocle de Mon Oncle

"Mother of heaven, regina of the clouds,
O sceptre of the sun, crown of the moon,
There is not nothing, no, no, never nothing,
Like the clashed edges of two words that kill."
And so I mocked her in magnificent measure.
Or was it that I mocked myself alone? (C.P. 13)

(I)

§ 58   The four-line quotation with which "Le Monocle" begins is presumably one from a poem Stevens wrote at some earlier time. The lines are an inflation of the rhetoric and diction Stevens used to address his Interior Paramour in "To the One of Fictive Music." "There is not nothing, no, no, never nothing like the clashed edges of two words that kill" can be praise for the imaginative faculty only if we read "kill" in a colloquial sense, as meaning "excite." The lines then say that the language of great poetry establishes relationships and tensions that give the reader a knowledge not otherwise attainable. But in their use of the double negatives these lines also seem to deflate the pretentions of poetry. Stevens is at once proud of his ability to poise the double attitude towards the Imagination so precisely, and a little dismayed by his own cuteness. For if the Imagination and its productions ("choirs") be mocked, what has the skeptical

139

poet left? Out of the Will and Desire in the poet for order
and color in life come fictions, the "radiant bubbles" that
burst when thoughts from a more bitter, ironic side of the
poet well up in his mind.[1] Thoughts of mortal decay and
death spoil the pleasure of the flights of the Imagination.
Only if flesh were stone could the mind give itself up completely to an imaginative mundo for longer than the
irrational moment. The poem of metaphors about the
moment, like "Le Monocle," is paradoxically always also
about the mind's rejection of the moment.

The poem as a whole, this complex, disjointed, brilliant
poem, plays with paradoxes: there is the paradox of a man
getting too old for physical love, yet feeling like a young
lover through a revelation concerning "true" love, love for
the "interior paramour"—the faith of a man of forty in the
joy emanating from the creative self. There is the paradox
of this love's being, in fact, a necessary coupling, desperate
romance, of the mortal self with blank reality, the eternal
basic slate. These paradoxes are refashioned over and over
again, in different figurations. There is little or no progression
in the poem; the twelve masterful sections can, in fact, easily
be read as separate entities.

(II)

Stevens' double vision is brilliantly figured in section two:

1. Note the same double attitude towards the Imagination (the
    "man with the blue guitar") in these lines using the "bubble"
    figure:
    > It may be the future depends on an orator,
    > Some pebble-chewer practiced in Tyrian speech,
    > An apparition, twanging instruments
    > Within us hitherto unknown, he that
    > Confounds all opposites and spins a sphere
    > Created, like a bubble, of bright sheens,
    > With a tendency to bulge as it floats away. (O.P. 63)

I am a man of fortune greeting heirs;
For it has come that thus I greet the spring.
These choirs of welcome choir for me farewell. (C.P. 13)

The aging uncle's offspring are poems, or, at least, the
creative, poetic instinct, that mood of "spring," which turns
the winds to "choirs of welcome." He is thus a man of
"fortune." But he is also a man of poverty, who is decaying,
and whose poems sing of his mortality within reality: "These
choirs of welcome choir for me farewell." Reality, the red
bird (see § 2), "seeks out his choir," or, in prose logic, the
poet seeks to make a choir out of reality's motions, out of
wind, rain, and flying birds (see § 39). The last two lines of
this section are addressed once again to the interior paramour, the poet's second self. The poet marvels that despite
all the fears of mortality and the assaults of reason, imaginative desire still wells up within one as inevitably as spring
comes. (Though, of course, irony is implied in a bliss that
comes from "anecdotes," and "making believe." Stevens
does not falsify his product, but the bliss, he insists, is real.)

(III)

The third section focuses on past "braidings" of reality
and then, in the last two lines, lauds the imagination that
continues to mythologize in an age of unbelief. The stanza
has already been discussed in § 27. The real world is without
a real curl, but no matter, the imagination will dream on this
nothingness, if only by instinct for self-preservation. The
imaginative mundo is, to be sure, a fabrication about reality,
but it is a conscious fiction; it does not pretend to encompass
a higher reality, as did myths of other times.

(IV)

The fruit of life, figured in the apple, and also the fruit of love, are tasted and enjoyed in youth out of simple desire, without reflection or study. It is at forty, when nature is seen to be without a curl, and when the body, like the apple, decays, that the imaginative meditation upon reality and the nature of love becomes necessary. This is the cycle of life for man, from tasting to thinking. The apple has its cycles too ("an apple serves as well as any skull to be the book in which to read a round"). The real apple is both luscious and acrid, as are all things of the world, but it is "impeccable," without taboo. When "Eve" was part of the imaginative myth people lived by, the "apple" was peccant, and went untasted, but—and Stevens is honest here—the sweetness of belief in an absolute nourished man then. The earthly paradise is no garden of uncontaminated bliss. The apple is composed of the same decaying matter that skulls are. The world is only "body," and this final knowledge is a maddening hardly tolerable lesson to learn. But we make of life what we can, taste of the sweet and acrid apple, and finally write fictions about it. To meditate on the skull rather than the apple is to live constantly within the fears of personal mortality to the exclusion of all the limited joy the sensual and the imaginative life can give.

(V)

Stevens compares two kinds of love in Stanza V. Fiery young men follow the furiously burning star of physical love. But like all things in the west, that star will set, and the impulse towards the physical will dwindle to the intensity of the firefly's stroke. But the new love for the creative imagination then takes over to give at times the appearance of meaning, life, and order to the dead earth. Both perishing personal love and the later love for the interior paramour are alike in that they give imaginary life to their worlds. And:

> The measure of the intensity of love
> Is measure, also, of the verve of earth.

"Verve" is precise. It is defined in Webster as "excitement of imagination and feeling attending artistic production; artistic enthusiasm." The fiery boys have their imaginations excited, but they are left with little at forty. Only by a new love then, for the imagination, can the real earth take on verve.

For Stevens' physical self, the time has grown tedious. For his imaginative self, the woman of Will and Desire within him, the prospects of life are not so unreservedly grey (though greyer here than in other stanzas). She can at least sing a chant of life's monotony:

> To hear only what one hears, one meaning alone,
> As if the paradise of meaning ceased
> To be paradise, it is this to be destitute.
> This is the sky divested of its fountains.
> Here in the west indifferent crickets chant
> Through our indifferent crises. Yet we require
> Another chant, an incantation, as in
> Another and later genesis. (C.P. 320–1)

The plea is for a belief in the illusions of metaphor, the making of music and meaning out of the chant of indifferent crickets (who figure the dry sound and dry body of reality). It is the Imagination's faculty to make one feel kin to the crickets, to establish fictive relations of man to exterior reality, when the only literally true kinship of man to cricket is that they both decay and die.

(VI)

Reality is a meaningless ocean of objects and motions which the artist draws upon to create his own calm and peaceful "lake" (§ 7). The painting of lakes represents the acceptance of illusion for its own sake, the coloring of life which is grey (slate) without it. There is a substance in us, beyond belief in myth, that prevails, and that is the desire, the rage for order. Stevens is aware that such statements are the minimum justification of the imaginative life, and indeed, his ironic image of the artist as middle-aged dilettante at the lakeshore further complicates for us his attitudes towards poetry in this poem. In the realization that there is nothing else, the illusions of youth (physical love) and the illusions of middle age (love of the Imagination) must be cultivated. The middle-aged amorist (the student of love) observes the fiery amours of youth and finds them but the caprices of random, transient ego-desires. The amorist is "bald" (without "curls"), the physical life is past; love for him must be of the sort that the unaccompanied exile must cultivate. He must lecture to himself, loving the creative faculty within himself. Apollo, the god of poetry, slew by accident his lover Hyacinth, the fair young boy, and wept. Stevens, a poet rather alienated from personal relations, likewise weeps for the loss of coherence and value that could give life and love a permanence they do not appear to have.

(VII)

Stanza VII renders some rather ambiguous attitudes of Stevens towards the religious imagination, and perhaps, in a submerged way, towards the poetic imagination also. There is a fairly simple reading of this stanza with which I expect most readers will agree. But there is much in Stevens' later poetry to make one wonder whether there is not a great deal more latent in this stanza than appears on the surface.

The parable seems to be a satire on two sorts of people. Religious people believe in a transcendant truth ("from beyond the sun"), and wait for the consummation of the revelation. Others, the unimaginative people, live completely in a sensual sty. The religious will probably never have their consummation, and the unimaginative will never be able to catch the moment's beauty in a creative act. Such a reading is all very well, but then are not the final two lines a bit flat? The poet creates a fiction, a damsel like Susanna (the honey of earth), that is admittedly impermanent; the religious feel *their* myth embodies an eternal truth, and perhaps, Stevens says, they are right. How does Stevens mean these last lines to be taken? I can only offer in answer some observations concerning the turn of Stevens' mind in his later poetry, when he returns to figures similar to those in the parable.

The only angels in Stevens' world are those necessary angels of the earth, poems of the real woven out of the imagination:

> I am the angel of reality,
> Seen for a moment standing in the door.
>
> I am the necessary angel of earth,
> Since, in my sight, you see the earth again. (C.P. 496)

The only heaven in Stevens' universe is the imaginative mundo composed of falsifying imagery which goes "beyond the sun" (phenomena) to represent the poet's desire (the palm):

> The palm at the end of the mind,
> Beyond the last thought, rises
> In the bronze distance. (O.P. 117)

The mountain in Stevens is a figure for the real which cannot be avoided by the poet, nor yet be endured without the Imagination. In another, later parable, Stevens has the complete realist, Mrs. Alfred Uruguay, riding up the mountain, and a poet, perhaps, riding down:

> The moonlight crumbled to degenerate forms,
> While she approached the real, upon her mountain,
> With lofty darkness. The donkey was there to ride,
> To hold by the ear, even though it wished for a bell,
> Wished faithfully for a falsifying bell.
>
> Who was it passed her there on a horse all will,
> What figure of capable imagination?
>
> [The rider] rode down the road,
> And, capable, created in his mind,
> Eventual victor, out of the martyrs' bones,
> The ultimate elegance: the imagined land.   (C.P. 249–50)

There is a tension in this characterization of the rider—the end of his journey down the mountain is an elegant, completely imaginary world of the mind. The muleteers in "Le Monocle" likewise are "dainty of their way" through the passes. What I am suggesting is that the muleteers could represent poets too. As an ironic undertone, Stevens might be allowing that the poets' occupation is, in ways, as pathetic as the religious thinker's. The damsel they both seek (permanence for the self, or for poetry) is probably not in the train.

(VIII)

The next two stanzas (VIII and IX) contrast again the two disparate attitudes of Stevens, those extremes in mood of acedia and euphoria towards the capacity of poetry to sustain the decaying poet. Uproarious sexual imagery begins in Stanza VIII and carries on through Stanza XI. Stanza VIII focuses bawdily on the physical body and the grotesqueness of its decay. Even the poet's inamorata, his imagination, though fecund till the death of the mind, will not, of course, outlast his body. The figure of the gourds in the weather is beautifully carried through; the passage is clear and beyond commentary.

(IX)

Stevens' hymn of oblation to the poetic imagination in Stanza IX is patently not without mockery. The figure of the skillful soldiers in war extends the lines in the first stanza: "There is not nothing, no, no, never nothing like the clashed edges of two words that kill." War is ridiculous and yet fated; poetry to the jaundiced eye is no less ridiculous, full of bravura and theatrical noises, but it does give life the verve that once religion supplied. Man used to fight and die for the Faith. The same sort of blind love and devotion is spent in the stanza on the imaginative act.[2] The venerable heart of the poet is yet a youth, a ward of cupido. Conceits can be broadened if women's bellies no longer can. Without belief in religious absolutes, or in the rational process and its formulations about reality, the poet can quiz all sounds, all thoughts, in order to make music from life. This being Stevens' catholic ideal for poetry, it is easy to appreciate the disjointed pattern of the poem—a series of random variations on the same themes, an attempt at rendering by vivid and concrete images radically different moods and perspectives on the same grey set of ideas about reality.

2. See the figure of the "soldier" at "war," § 9.

(X)

The "fops of fancy" are poets who, even more audacious than philosophers, believe they can transcend phenomena (our gritty soil). They fulfill their desire for cosmic order by the simple assertion that it exists, a process akin to masturbation. Stevens is a less pretentious cultivator of the reality around him. He does not believe in the possibility of transcendance, in magic, mythy boughs, or, say, Gerard Hopkins' gold-vermilion fruit which may figure forth a divine message. He sees a tree, not as something magical, but as a figure for an object "tipped" (a phallic tree) or to be "tipped" by that slight imaginative distortion that allows Fictions to be made.[3] A given Fiction, like sexual desire, waxes and wanes, but the real object (here the "tree" that figures both) is still there. The faith of forty is in the object and the beneficence of the illusions to be fathered upon it.

(XI)

Sex, the act of love, serves here as a figure also for the imaginative performance by the lover of poetry. If sex were all, that is, if one's allegiance to the "truth" of things were not a necessary part of love for the Imagination, then the poems of the fops of fancy would suffice for the mind desirous of order. The poet, however, must be faithful to the real, even though his fate within it is to die. Death is the first, foremost law of reality; the poet is repaid by death for the verve he gives to the earth. The whole poetic process can seem absurd in this light, and is compared to the more comic side of the physical efforts in the act of love. Or, in another figuration, the poet is shown in the absurd but neces-

3. Compare "Bantams in Pine-Woods." See also § 12.

sary position of creating the order of the lily pond, only to
have the odious belly sound of the frog destroy the illusion.

(XII)

We have spoken earlier in this study (§ 39) of the flight
of birds—how, in Stevens' figuration, curved, controlled
motion represents an imaginative integration of simple perceptions. But inevitably a fictional mundo grows insipid, and
a return to the facts of perception is necessary, the bird can
no longer fly:

> A blue pigeon it is, that circles the blue sky,
> On sidelong wing, around and round and round.
> A white pigeon it is, that flutters to the ground,
> Grown tired of flight. (C.P. 17)

It is still the same reality, whether seen as red, or blue, or
white; it is still that which is external to us. But our imaginative perception of it makes all the difference to us, to our
moods and attitudes. It is as if the mind puts colored filters
before our eyes. With a dark filter through which to view
phenomena, the world looks dark, and the mind will be
harsh in its estimate of mankind. A blue, or white, or rose
filter will alter our estimation of the world and of man's
situation within it. Mankind, man's fate, seen without the
creative imagination is dark. At forty the revelation of the
Imagination as Value comes to the scholarly uncle (now a
rabbi in rose) and he pursues the vagaries of his paramour
by perceiving the light, color and motion in the real world,
until the red bird becomes the blue bird.

One *must* imagine the blue bird, for reality gives nothing
like satisfaction to desire. One must have a dream in face of
the object. This is the sober point beneath all of Stevens'

poetry. There is a draft of a poem in *Opus Posthumous*, obviously intended to counterpoint "Le Monocle de Mon Oncle" called "The Naked Eye of My Aunt." The aunt is one who tries to face the object too squarely. The result is frightening:

> Eheu! Eheu! With what a weedy face
> Black fact emerges from her swishing dreams.   (O.P. 19)

What then is this "monocle" that the uncle wears, through which he perceives? It would seem to me obviously a glass that allows for "revealing aberrations" to be imposed on reality, for those imaginative distortions of the perceived world that enable one to face the object. It is perhaps pretentious for Mon Oncle to wear a monocle but it is the role that our time (without a curl so far as he can see) forces him to play. Gaiety must be wrenched from words and dreams; his choirs of love must find their final response in his own, his aging self.

Chapter Nine

The Comedian as the Letter C

§ 59   "The Comedian as the Letter C" is a poem whose surface is composed of a stream, a torrent of figures "delivered with a deluging outwardness." This surface is perhaps impenetrable in matters of local detail if it is approached without some acquaintance with Stevens' figuration.[1] One of the original purposes of this study was to explicate the "Comedian" with some precision and sensitivity to the complex attitudes beneath the surface. I propose to look at the whole Section I of the poem and thereafter at what seems to me the most difficult lines of the following sections.

One general point first. The poem, a spiritual autobiography of Stevens, and, by extension, of the poetic consciousness of western man in modern times, is intended to have a definite dramatic and doctrinal progression. Each section represents a new step in Crispin's mind towards the final formulations of Section VI; Crispin is treated with an affectionate irony till then. Each section contains lines which represent formulations by Crispin that we are to read ironically since, for Stevens, they are only partially right. Other lines in each section are straightforward commentary by Stevens on Crispin. Stevens, of course, is characteristically

1.   Particularly good on the "Comedian" are Simons, O'Connor, Blackmur, Fuchs, and Kermode. See Bibliography.

ironic, but sometimes to others and their formulations, and at other times to himself and his doctrines. It is obviously important to try to distinguish one sort of irony from the other.

I. THE WORLD WITHOUT IMAGINATION

> Nota: man is the intelligence of his soil,
> The sovereign ghost. As such, the Socrates
> Of snails, musician of pears, principium
> And lex.

Man, in his villages, has for centuries cultivated the land about him, and has lorded it over nature, thinking himself its *raison d'etre,* the spirit of the world's body. (Similarly, once ghosts were thought spirits who had existence outside of our minds.)[2] Objects supposedly existed for the use of man. This attitude was Crispin's once, that "ancient Crispin of Bordeaux" (European man of a few centuries back).

> Sed quaeritur: is this same wig
> Of things, this nincompated pedagogue,
> Preceptor to the sea? Crispin at sea
> Created, in his day, a touch of doubt.

"Land" represents the solid foundation of things back in Bordeaux; the sea figures the vast chaos of experiences that tells man that he is not at the center of things. To wear a wig is a pretentious eighteenth-century thing to do; only a nincompoop would pretend to the authoritative knowledge implicit in putting one on his pate. One must keep one's eye on the real "hairs" in the world (these distortions of the

---

2. For "ghosts" see § 10. The first fifteen lines of the "Comedian" have already been examined in § 26.

actual inherent in the perceiving eye which make it impossible to know "reality," and, also, those deliberate distortions of the imaginative eye).[3] Later (in Section VI, "And Daughters With Curls") Crispin will in fact make "coiffures" or "braidings" out of the inscrutable hair of the perceived world. The "wig" (imaginings not rooted in perception) made man feel himself the ruler of things. Crispin, novice poet, incipient iconoclast, creates a "touch" (renders in poetry the mood) of doubt.

> An eye most apt in gelatines and jupes,
> Berries of villages, a barber's eye,
> An eye of land, of simple salad-beds,
> Of honest quilts, the eye of Crispin, hung
> On porpoises, instead of apricots,
> And on silentious porpoises, whose snouts
> Dibbled in waves that were mustachios,
> Inscrutable hair in an inscrutable world.

The ancient Crispin had woven a wholly imaginary world (represented by the "honest quilt") out of his own earnest desire for order. His world was composed of the things around him in his land, berries and apricots and the like. Crispin was like a barber, clipping and caring for a wig of his own creation, a world in (or on) his brain. But modern man has seen sea animals that the good people of Bordeaux never saw before.

Now the existence of the sea of objects is no less a mystery than it ever was; the porpoise has a "mustache." The waves, by extension, are too mustachioed. Still, this inscrutable world of objects coldly perceived (with a salt eye) does not speak to us of our centrality in the universe anymore. The

3. For "hair," "curls," "beards," "coiffures," "braids," "twists," etc., see § 26.

world is a lumpy *paté* (meat pie) which we must swallow as it is: "One eats one's paté, even of salt, quotha."[4] The pun on paté is obvious; one eats one's head, so to speak, when old beliefs and old formulations are swallowed up by the sea.

> It was not so much the lost terrestrial,
> The snug hibernal from that sea and salt,
> That century of wind in a single puff.
> What counted was mythology of self,
> Blotched out beyond unblotching. Crispin,
> The lutanist of fleas, the knave, the thane,
> The ribboned stick, the bellowing breeches, cloak
> Of China, cap of Spain, imperative haw
> Of hum, inquisitorial botanist,
> And general lexicographer of mute
> And maidenly greenhorns, now beheld himself,
> A skinny sailor peering in the sea-glass.

§ 60   Lost was the land, refuge where warm winds dallied for centuries. The sea wind is cold and salty and blows with one monotonous and inhuman sound, which has nothing of the sounds of our miseries.[5] The ancient Crispin represents the transcendental poet of many times and places who attempted to make order out of reality by falsifying it. He wove cloaks and caps, breeches and ribbons to embellish a reality of sticks and fleas.[6] He made a false transcendent music ("haw of hum"); imperatives within him (Will and Desire) demanded he say something absolute and axiomatic (as "inquisitorial botanist" and "general lexicographer") about the inscrutable green world (a maiden who will not

4.   Compare the 'Turnip" figure in Section VI, and see also § 18.
5.   For this sound, see § 24.
6.   For various sorts of "drapery" to figure the imaginative embell-
      ishment of "naked" reality, see § 40. For "cap," see § 41.

speak). Truth is, we can only observe, not explain the sea
or the land.

> What word split up in clickering syllables
> And storming under multitudinous tones
> Was name for this short-shanks in all that brunt?

No word really. Just a letter is more like it. The letter "c"
taken from his name expresses correctly his insignificance
(short shanks, lower case, minuscule letter) in contrast to
the real (magnitude, upper case, the large).

> Crispin was washed away by magnitude.
> The whole of life that still remained in him
> Dwindled to one sound strumming in his ear,
> Ubiquitous concussion, slap and sigh,
> Polyphony beyond his baton's thrust.

The one monotonous sound of the sea is ironically too poly-
phonic to be handled in the poet's music.

> Could Crispin stem verboseness in the sea,
> The old age of a watery realist,
> Triton, dissolved in shifting diaphanes
> Of blue and green?

In ages past the shifting diaphanes of the sea caused man,
full of religious awe and imagination, to create Triton. If the
figure is to be used at all in our age, we must picture Triton
(the sea) as a senile old babbler roaring without sense, the
apparition constantly dissolving back into the real waves
from which it sprung.

> A wordy, watery age
> That whispered to the sun's compassion, made
> A convocation, nightly, of the sea-stars,
> And on the clopping foot-ways of the moon
> Lay grovelling.

Our age can pray or chant to, or go on a pilgrimage for, not the mythic gods we used to create from sun, moon, and stars, but only the natural objects themselves. The irony in our grovelling before inanimate objects is intentional on Stevens' part.

> Triton incomplicate with that
> Which made him Triton, nothing left of him,
> Except in faint, memorial gesturings,
> That were like arms and shoulders in the waves,
> Here, something in the rise and fall of wind
> That seemed hallucinating horn, and here,
> A sunken voice, both of remembering
> And of forgetfulness, in alternate strain.

All that is left for the once mighty god is memory, hallucination, fits of forgetfulness, futile gesturings and bellowings. This is all that is left of the mythologies of the past, and, all that is left of man bereft of the myths which made him master of the sea.

> Just so an ancient Crispin was dissolved
> The valet in the tempest was annulled.
> Bordeaux to Yucatan, Havana next,
> And then to Carolina. Simple jaunt.
> Crispin, merest minuscule in the gales,
> Dejected his manner to the turbulence.[7]

The introspective voyager must leave the old world (figured as Europe, Bordeaux, the East) for the new (America, the West). But which America? Both are in the West and both presumably would serve the European. The choice is one of temperament, and the differences between the Americas of the South and of the North will be the sub-

7. For "tempest" and "gale," see § 23.

ject of sections II and III. Crispin is cut down (dejected) to
lower case, a mere minuscule. At such a low point in Crispin's career, we enter his mind to learn his attitude towards
his predicament:

> The salt hung on his spirit like a frost,
> The dead brine melted in him like a dew
> Of winter, until nothing of himself
> Remained, except some starker, barer self
> In a starker, barer world, in which the sun
> Was not the sun because it never shone
> With bland complaisance on pale parasols,
> Beetled, in chapels, on the chaste bouquets.

§ 61   The dead brine is the encrustation of old mythologies of the sea spray. The "dew of winter" is an oxymoron:
the old mythologies are of another season, but were "dew"
once. The new brine, the real salt air is no less frosty, but
Crispin exults in his new self. He feels he sees the sun
(phenomena) as a realist, not as a sentimentalist, the sun
is not the benign servant of man, embellishing his "bouquets"
(see § 30) or giving opportunity to genteel ladies to bring out
their "para-sols."

Crispin is perhaps a little too cocksure here and is chas-
tized: "against his pipping sounds a trumpet cried celestial
sneering boisterously." The trumpet of the real (not Triton's
hallucinating horn) announces to Crispin that the sun in
the bare sky beats down on him also, and that he will want
the shadow of a parasol (or "nice shady home") someday,
like everyone else. But this is in the future.

> Crispin
> Became an introspective voyager.

> Here was the veritable ding an sich, at last,

> Crispin confronting it, a vocable thing,
> But with a speech belched out of hoary darks
> Noway resembling his, a visible thing,
> And excepting negligible Triton, free
> From the unavoidable shadow of himself
> That lay elsewhere around him.

Ironically, Crispin is introspective in that he is depending at last, not on inherited mythologies of nature, but on his own perceptions of the *outer* visible reality (the "ding an sich" or object alone). The sea of objects belches dark, meaningless sounds. Poems that Crispin might now write would have a harmony that resembles nothing in nature since poems produce "shadows" (relief for the sun-burnt spirit) which do not exist in nature, but only in the poet's irrepressible Will ("elsewhere around him"). Nature is free of the shadows man's imagination imposes on it, free even of the skeptical poet's minimum distortion, the "negligible Triton" described above.

> Severance
> Was clear. The last distortion of romance
> Forsook the insatiable egotist. The sea
> Severs not only lands but also selves.
> Here was no help before reality
> Crispin beheld and Crispin was made new.

Crispin is very strict at this stage. The poem is a fiction about reality; the imaginative self of the poet is a romancier about a reality which the rationalist self sees hard and clear. The two selves are separate, and always at war;[8] each has its own characteristic vision. The realist feels this way:

8. The imaginative self fighting back against reality and the skeptical self, is figured as the "soldier at war." See § 9.

> The imagination, here, could not evade,
> In poems of plums, the strict austerity
> Of one vast, subjugating, final tone.
> The drenching of stale lives no more fell down.

The modern poet, it is clear, should not make music about plums (which would picture the world as sweet fruit) and evade the blankness of nature. Nor should he depend on stale mythologies to bring down spiritual rain (§ 23) to parched lives.

But the imaginative eye looks at the world and makes something of it anyway, without a mythology, simply through a desire for Order:

> What was this gaudy, gusty panoply?
> Out of what swift destruction did it spring?
> It was caparison of wind and cloud
> And something given to make whole among
> The ruses that were shattered by the large.

Out of wind and cloud, sea and sun, blank phenomena, the imagination creates a panoply, saddles the world and holds the reins.[9] The will to do so springs from the desire to make a whole, or some semblance of an order, out of "the large" (see above), the monstrous reality. The modern perception of the real has shattered all our old ruses, those tricks we played on ourselves in the past for the sake of order.

§ 62   There is no attempt in Section I to reconcile the two conflicting visions or selves in the poet, and we feel moreover two different attitudes towards the conflict.

9. Compare "Notes towards a Supreme Fiction" II: 10, where the west wind is controlled by "a will to make iris frettings on the blank" (with a word-play on "iris").

Crispin has yet to experience the full force of the modern disinheritance, and is rather condescending to the imagination's "evasions" of reality. Stevens is more humble. He has been through Crispin's experiences and knows that one *must* "have a dream in face of the object," and that the dream is blessed. It is now perhaps worthwhile to attempt to outline what happens to Crispin's attitudes in the following five sections.

Sections II and III show the impossibility of living completely "in face of the object," either in a southern environment, or in a northern one. Section IV attempts to review Crispin's experiences in the two hemispheres, and to present the sum of his mid-wisdom. Crispin is represented as still suspicious of "moonlight" and dreams, preferring "text to gloss." He is too certain about the ability of each perceiving mind to know the one and the same reality (and thus form a "colony"), he is still serving "grotesque apprenticeship to chance event." Section V renders Crispin's slow awareness that each mind perceives a different reality, that each man's perceived reality is in fact tinged by the "blue-infected will" in the very moment of perception, that no colony of minds can write poems of the very same reality, that each man's mind is a "hermit" ruled by his will and desire for order. Each man must be satisfied with his own "nice shady home," his "cabin," where he dreams the dreams of his subjective mind. Once the modern poet is thus humbled, his attitude towards the distortions of poetry ("Daughters with Curls") changes; he is no longer condescending, but worshipful towards the imagination's moonshine. This humility rather than disdain towards imaginative "fictions" enables Crispin to be comedian rather than tragedian about life.

II. CONCERNING THE THUNDERSTORMS OF YUCATAN

When Crispin gets to the Yucatan he finds indigenous poets who are romantics, or transcendentalists, who face the object no more than did his European confreres (they pray to the "nightbird"). Crispin had once written romantic poems of smooth "parks," but now his perception is "desperately clear;" he sees the real rucks of the actual earth. Now a "freeman" bound to no mythology, he is like an empty shell. He at first has confidence that he can write poems that deal with quintessential fact alone, the elemental "rock" or "mountain" of reality (§ 25). He assumes he can make music of the "Andean breath." This is not so. He can, however, make poems of the *differences* in the exotic ("fabulous"), savage southern landscape from other landscapes, poems of "secondary things" on the mountain, not of the mountain itself.[10]

> The fabulous and its intrinsic verse
> Came like two spirits parleying, adorned
> In radiance from the Atlantic coign,
> For Crispin and his quill to catechize.
> But they came parleying of such an earth,
> So thick with sides and jagged lops of green,
> So intertwined with serpent-kin encoiled
> Among the purple tufts, the scarlet crowns,
> Scenting the jungle in their refuges,
> So streaked with yellow, blue and green and red
> In beak and bud and fruity gobbet-skins,
> That earth was like a jostling festival
> Of seeds grown fat, too juicily opulent,
> Expanding in the gold's maternal warmth.

10. For Stevens' concept of secondary things, see "Man Carrying Thing," "Credences of Summer," IV, and § 7.

             . . . The affectionate emigrant found
    A new reality in parrot-squawks.

In other words, the poems of the Yucatan were Yucatan poems, depicting its efflorescence, not its essence, its South Atlantic flora and fauna, not a universal reality. No voyager or poet ("annotator") can depict that. The real wind blows over a totality that no poem of the Yucatan can render, as the bassoon's part is nothing compared to the music of the whole orchestra. The "valet" cannot own this thing; real thunder and lightning are not represented in any significant way by the signboard's trembling, or by a flash in a window pane. The scrupulous voyager will go no further "west" in an attempt to reach the "Andes;" he can only go North if he does not feel at home in the South.

III.   APPROACHING CAROLINA

Stevens comments detachedly on Crispin in the opening stanza of this section. Crispin is not even halfway in his "pilgrimage through sweating changes;" he is still a "sophomore;" he considers "moonlight" (imaginative fictions) as perhaps "wrong as a divagation to Peking." Still, Stevens asserts, his poems are honest, and he will find his place in the never-to-be-finished "book of moonlight." His poems of North America (Carolina) are in fact poems of moonlight, though perhaps he did not intend them to be. His mind was necessarily always "above," not on the continent; what he *had* done was to find a congenial environment in the North, and his imagination made an order out of it. (Whether one writes of North or South, the Andean or the Arctic breath, is a matter of temperament, or perhaps, exposure).[11] But

11. For "North" and "South" in Stevens, see § 15.

Crispin had wanted to grasp the quintessence, the "text," the vulgar "prose" (the "vulgate") of his northern environment, and could not do so. He is at this point rather ashamed of what he did accomplish in his poems.

> It [the arctic moonlight] seemed
> Illusive, faint, more mist than moon, perverse,
> Wrong as a divagation to Peking,
> To him that postulated as his theme
> The vulgar, as his theme and hymn and flight,
> A passionate niggling nightingale.
> Moonlight was an evasion, or, if not,
> A minor meeting, facile, delicate.
> Thus he conceived his voyaging to be
> An up and down between two elements,
> A fluctuating between sun and moon,
> A sally into gold and crimson forms,
> As on this voyage, out of goblinry,
> And then retirement like a turning back
> And sinking down to the indulgences
> That in the moonlight have their habitude.
> But let these backward lapses, if they would,
> Grind their seductions on him, Crispin knew
> It was a flourishing tropic he required
> For his refreshment, an abundant zone,
> Prickly and obdurate, dense, harmonious,
> Yet with a harmony not rarefied
> Nor fined for the inhibited instruments
> Of over-civil stops. And thus he tossed
> Between a Carolina of old time,
> A little juvenile, an ancient whim,
> And the visible, circumspect presentment drawn
> From what he saw across his vessel's prow.

He accepts his recurring need for moonlight, for a "Carolina of old time," as a "refreshment," an "indulgence," but he is embarrassed by his need when he looks out at the sea or sun which his poetry cannot encompass. But, Crispin feels at least his poetry is *conscious* moonshine based on a perceived reality, and not rarified myth about a supernatural passionately believed in.

However, it is precisely this reluctance about giving oneself up wholly to the imaginative moment that is wrong in Crispin. He rejects rightly mythic projections of man as the world's ruler, but he cannot respond wholeheartedly to the spring:

> He came. The poetic hero without palms
> Or jugglery, without regalia.
> And as he came he saw that it was spring,
> A time abhorrent to the nihilist
> Or searcher for the fecund minimum.
> The moonlight fiction disappeared. The spring,
> Although contending featly in its veils,
> Irised in dew and early fragrancies,
> Was gemmy marionette to him that sought
> A sinewy nakedness.

Stevens is saying that an imaginative response to the (veiled) world is instinctive and is as much a part of our being as our rational response.[12] To consider it an "indulgence" or a "lapse" is self-defeating. Crispin, in "spring," is even more sensitive to the characteristically northern landscapes than he was to the southern, but he rests in these as the "one integrity for him," when in fact he will come to see that an imaginative integration, or poetic vision of the world, is another. He discovers that "prose" indeed does "wear a poem's guise at last."

12. Stevens often speaks of the imaginative "moment" when the mind feels with an inexplicable joy that it has encompassed the world: see § 68. For "drapery" and "nakedness," see § 40.

IV.   THE IDEA OF A COLONY

The *nota* that begins this section is but a half-truth, for man must not only stick to what he sees (though this is the first step in the poetic process); he can dream on what he sees. Crispin is too preemptory in tossing out moonlight, in presuming that poets could, all together, grasp the essential prose of reality so that each might write poems about the parcel of reality he knew best (in a "colony").

Crispin's "first central hymns" were purposely extreme in their iconoclasm, disdaining the old poetry and its (transcendant) vision, celebrating a new poetry of pure, naked perception. He felt his western voyage had ended with the discovery of this new poetry and new aesthetic: "The natives of the rain are rainy men . . . their azure has a cloudy edge." Each poet, that is, should write only of what his perception has instructed him; the gross red Indian should not speak of gold, nor the Eskimo pose as Turk. This, of course, is far too doctrinaire; the imagination here is too confined. The lines beginning "Upon these premises propounding . . ." and ending "shrewd novitiates should be the clerks of our experience" clearly and bewitchingly render Crispin's mind on these matters. Crispin is pictured so sensitive to the distortions of perception inherent in metaphor that he can hardly bear any sort of poetry at all. "Afflatus," "counterfeit," "masquerade of thought," "hapless words," "fictive flourishes," "trash"—this is how one skeptical side of Crispin's mind thinks of poetry. Crispin prefers "text" to "gloss" in this period of "grotesque apprenticeship to chance event." There is a truth that he is yet to learn, about the irrepressibility of the imaginative instinct within us. He is still fighting the instinct:

> There is a monotonous babbling in our dreams
> That makes them our dependent heirs, the heirs
> Of dreamers buried in our sleep, . . .
> The apprentice knew these dreamers. If he dreamed
> Their dreams, he did it in a gingerly way.
> All dreams are vexing. Let them be expunged.

The dreamers buried in our sleep (our unconscious) are Will and Desire (§ 8). They have no metaphysical or supersensory knowledge, but they demand that the mind which serves them live often in imaginative mundos. The mundo's untruth is vexing to Crispin:

> But let the rabbit run, the cock declaim.
>
> Trinket pasticcio, flaunting skyey sheets,
> With Crispin as the tiptoe cozener?
> No, no: veracious page on page, exact.

Crispin still wants to face the object (the "cock") in his poems rather than to string artificial beads, or write transcendant lyrics ("skyey sheets") wherein one lies to oneself. He admits no middle-ground.

V.   A NICE SHADY HOME

For a while Crispin lives thus as "prickling realist," not realizing that his poems (his "chits") were like all poems "confect," and "cloudy" as they must be. But he changes:

> Crispin dwelt in the land and dwelling there
> Slid from his continent by slow recess
> To things within his actual eye, alert
> To the difficulty of rebellious thought
> When the sky is blue. The blue infected will.

The "actual eye" is not only the simple perceiving eye of
the poet, but also an imaginative eye of Will and Desire—the
total person viewing a total reality where the imaginative
ordering is as real as the simple perceiving. The will is
infected with a desire to make color of life. When the sky
is blue, or spring comes (when the imagination is functioning), skeptical thought holds no sway over the mind. The
white yarrow can look purple to the imagination, or appear
another color another day.

> It may be that the yarrow in his fields
> Sealed pensive purple under its concern.
> But day by day, now this thing and now that
> Confined him, while it cosseted, condoned,
> Little by little, as if the suzerain soil
> Abashed him by carouse to humble yet
> Attach. It seemed haphazard denouement.

All objects change and fluctuate ("carouse") in our imaginative perception of them. The realization (that perception is
not absolute) is a humbling one, but it makes one feel more
attachment to, less disdain for, the purple yarrow in the
mind.

Now a single given poem about the yarrow or the plum
will indeed indulge in obliquities about yarrow or plum, and
the plum does survive the poem. But

> Was he to bray this in profoundest brass
> Arointing his dreams with frugal requiems?

Must dreams be banished (arointed)? he is asking. Is it a
defeat that Crispin turns to "salad beds" again? The new
insight of Crispin is that it is not a tragic defeat, for he knows
now that

> The very man despising honest quilts
> Lies quilted to his poll in his despite.

The ancient Crispin back in Bordeaux wove an imaginative world for himself that the prickling realist despises, but the truth is that the weaving instinct is inherent to the mind. For realists, "what is is what should be," but for Crispin now, form can at times substitute for truth, the form of the real plum *or* the form of a poem about it.

> And so it came, his cabin shuffled up,
> His trees were planted, his duenna brought
> Her prismy blonde and clapped her in his hands,
> The curtains flittered and the door was closed.
> Crispin, magister of a single room,
> Latched up the night.[13]

Crispin at last makes the only possible accommodation between reality on the one hand and his will and desire on the other. He will set up house in a cabin (the mind), tend to his little garden (his poems). His duenna is the Will that guards his Imagination (the prismy blonde) from the sad fate of Tragedians and Realists. The Night is obscure, fearsome, inscrutable; each man is locked in the room which is his mind; the curtains (imaginative weavings) give form to the room and to the wind blowing through them. The sound of crickets in the wind outside do not drown out the inside music he makes. They are servants (custodians) of the real, he is magister of a single room (compare "The Final Soliloquy of The Interior Paramour").

Crispin is, to be sure, like the cricket, a grub within reality, but in his own room he keeps out the sun of the quotidian and counters philosophic despair. To "track the knaves of

13. For the mind as a room see § 7. For the "curtains," see § 43.

thought" is a fruitless endeavor; analysis always destroys. What is needed is fictive syntheses, compositions of the quotidian. Crispin's compositions are different from the old poetry, but compositions they are nonetheless. The rose in Crispin's poetry is not the "noble thorn, of crinoline spread" the way victorian poets might have seen the rose (and perhaps themselves). But the rose is still a "pining sweet," still a figure for the poet's own self, expressing at once Crispin's melancholy and also his love for his "interior paramour," the Imagination.

> He poured out upon the lips of her
> That lay beside him, the quotidian
> Like this, saps like the sun, true fortuner.
> For all it takes it gives a humped return
> Exchequering from piebald fiscs unkeyed.

What he pours out in words is the quotidian composed, ordered in "speech." "Saps" here is used in an opposite sense to "enervates" (compare above, "the quotidian saps philosophers"); the sun in this passage does not dry out the spirit but makes it flourish, makes its sap run. "This," the composition, is our true fortune in life. "It" gives back joy manifold for an investment in that inexhaustible (unkeyed) bank, the prismatic imagination (the "piebald fisc").

VI.   AND DAUGHTERS WITH CURLS

The section opens with an invocation to Sound (strange god) that Crispin's final pronouncements about poetry and the imaginative life be well stated. The poetry of his full maturity is described.

> The chits came for his jiggling, bluet-eyed,
> Hands without touch yet touching poignantly,

> Leaving no room upon his cloudy knee,
> Prophetic joint, for its diviner young.

These children of his desire are poems, intangibles of the spirit tinged with the imagination's blue. Since the mind is always "cloudy," his earlier poems, that aspired to absolute rendering of the real, have no place in his later world. Crispin has lost his arrogance, and fathered many "children nibbling at the sugared void, infants yet eminently old," borne them in his mind (figured as "dome and halidom for the unbraided femes"). The femes are fictions, their curls are the distorting revealing metaphors of poetry.[14] The infants are old because the poetic process is old and enduring; the need to make poetry out of life is our deepest need, and so the poems are "true daughters both of Crispin and his clay." Crispin had first been a romantic, then a colonizing realist and is now a fatalist. But he had not expected the spontaneous joy that in fact came from the products of his imagination (which, poignantly, are so perishable, so soon in need of "weathery rouges").

The four daughters represent for Stevens something like four different kinds of poem, from the most ambitious and self-conscious to the most trivially descriptive. The "goldenest demoiselle" figures the poem that deals most with the inscrutable world, that theorizes about the secret and singular world of the imagination. The second sister has not yet felt desire for the mundos of the imagination; she is still content to dream only about the local objects around her. The other two are not at all conscious of the need for the imaginative life.

> A few years more and the vermeil capuchin
> Gave to the cabin, lordlier than it was,

14. For "women," see § 22. For "braids" and "curls," see § 26.

The dulcet omen fit for such a house.
The second sister dallying was shy
To fetch the one full-pinioned one himself
Out of her botches, hot embosomer.

The eldest daughter made the cabin more lordly than it
was before by bringing forth (or placing in it) a child of the
imagination. The father for this integration is the Lord, the
"full-pinioned one"; he is the god in the temporary imaginative mundo of a poem (§ 42). This is the personage called
variously in other poems the "hero," the "major" or the
"mighty" man. The second sister longs for a lover, but does
not yet attempt the integration.

The third one gaping at the orioles
Lettered herself demurely as became
A pearly poetess, peaked for rhapsody.
The fourth, pent now, a digit curious.

The third daughter represents the poem (or the poet who
writes the poem) that has not gone beyond the act of perception of objects, and sings only of these (of pearl instead
of gold). The fourth merely looks (she is curious), she does
not write (she is "pent now"), she is but a number (a pun on
"pent") in reality, not a name or letter.

Four daughters in a world too intricate
In the beginning, four blithe instruments
Of differing struts, four voices several
In couch, four more personae, intimate
As buffo, yet divers, four mirrors blue
That should be silver, four accustomed seeds
Hinting incredible hues, four selfsame lights
That spread chromatics in hilarious dark,
Four questioners and four sure answerers.

The too intricate world can be handled only in the poem; the poet can write a poem from any of the four stances or perspectives or mental states that the four daughters represent. All give pleasure to poet and reader. The poem makes the world appear blue (the color desired) rather than the silver (monochrome) that it is. Poetry distorts but poetry pleases, makes the dark colorful and cheerful.

Once Crispin felt that reality was the same to all perceivers of it, a turnip readily plucked. Its "purples" (distortions of what it really is) could be "daubed out," and its essence could be understood once and for all. However Crispin has seen the world is not so easily known; it "came reproduced in purple, family font, the same insoluble lump." For generation after generation, for both ancient and modern Crispins, the turnip or the berry or the plum will remain tangible mysteries. And of these mysteries the imagination creates a fictive world. In his closing lines, Stevens makes no apologies for the imaginative process, though some may say that this final summation of experience ("autumn's compendium") is but intellectual cowardice, or illogic, or evasion. Crispin has come to believe that man must live not so much with his intellect, but with his feelings. Each man lives in a myth, caring for "curls" that give him some feeling of relation to the world of perception. The poet writes of these feelings:

> And so distorting, proving what he proves
> Is nothing, what can all this matter since
> The relation comes, benignly, to its end?
>
> So may the relation of each man be clipped.

Each man dies, each man's curl is clipped, and each man's tale (pun on "relation") is cut off, or has an end. No man has any relation to the world of things finally, but the poet at least has the intermittent joy of a fictive relationship. He is the intelligence of his world when he wills that he is.

Stevens is no longer ironic to Crispin; he is Crispin in these last pages; he is ironic only to himself now. Stevens drops the turnip "down his craw, without grace or grumble." The image is a comic one, and Stevens is finally a comedian, but in the diviner sense of the word, where a comic vision engages the poet in a deep and poignant drama with the world.

Chapter Ten

Credences of Summer

§ 63 "Credences of Summer" attempts to render the serenity of the imaginative moment, the time of equilibrium when "the mind lays by its troubles." But the attempt is not made so successfully as in, say, that last poem, "Of Mere Being" (see § 34). Everywhere there are evidences of a desperate battling with the mind's desire for permanence. Syntax and logical connection have been loosened so as to blur this separation between desire and achievement. Lovely and effective imagery from folk tale and a magical medieval setting tend to exaggerate the bliss in the poem.

> Now the mind lays by its trouble and considers.
> The fidgets of remembrance come to this.
> This is the last day of a certain year
> Beyond which there is nothing left of time.
> It comes to this and the imagination's life. (C.P. 372)

What is Stevens saying here? Why is it the last day of a certain year when it is supposedly midsummer? The passage is ominous, and yet why? The answer, it seems, is in Section V:

> One day enriches a year. One woman makes
> The rest look down. One man becomes a race,
> Lofty like him, like him perpetual.
> Or do the other days enrich the one?

174

The bristling soldier, weather-foxed, who looms
In the sunshine is a filial form and one
Of the land's children, easily born, its flesh,
Not fustian. The more than casual blue

Contains the year and other years and hymns
And people, without souvenir.   (C.P. 374–375)[1]

The "certain year" of section I is seen as a part of the heavy
load of living "place bound and time bound" (see C.P. 363),
in a burgherish, pitiful existence ("weather-foxed"). The "one
day" represents the imaginative moment, when physical and
personal desires are spent more profitably on the interior
paramour, when man and his personal problems are projected into a "Major Man" (see § 42). One must forget personal longings and desires of the self, the "fathers,"
"mothers," and "lovers" (C.P. 372). These are "false
disasters" because one can surmount the sorrow of their loss
through the imagination (see § 4). The shock in these lines
is deliberate. Stevens wants to dramatize the enormous
amount the modern mind has lost while retaining the minimum tranquility of the imagination.

There is a great deal of pathos in the following lines which
call for a realization that nature is barren, but that imaginative desire in man endures anyway:

Trace the gold sun about the whitened sky
Without evasion by a single metaphor.
Look at it in its essential barrenness
And say this, this is the centre that I seek.
Fix it in an eternal foliage

1. For "soldier," see § 9. The soldier is projected large in the
sunlight as the "hero" (see § 42). The projection is "flesh" (§ 43)
not "fustian" (§ 40).

> And fill the foliage with arrested peace,
> Joy of such permanence, right ignorance
> Of change still possible. Exile desire
> For what is not. (C.P. 373)[2]

To fix the foliage, to hold peace, to attain permanence, to be ignorant of change, all these are the objects of desire, and are impossible. Only metaphor can give even the illusion of such attainment.[3]

§ 64   The poem exhibits this paradox over and over again. The clarion call (VIII) is to see the visible only, say, the bean pole (IX), and to dispense with metaphor, "suave bush and polished beast." But only by the gaudiest metaphor, it seems, of tumblers and princes and dervishes can the poet make one feel for what he says. The essential barrenness of reality is figured as the "final mountain" or the "rock" (§ 25). The utmost the imagination can do is to fuse the "rock" with "good air," and this must be enough for us in our poverty. We must resign ourselves to ask no more: "The utmost must be good and is" (C.P. 374). It is, in fact, what the poet makes out of the "casual blue" and the "placid air" (C.P. 375), the metaphors he creates that matter. The "sapphires" we make from light and air, the "days" we fashion from disordered years, however, are not "souvenirs" (C.P. 375); they will not sustain us after the moment is gone. It takes an enormous force of will, an effort of concentration and renunciation (see VII), to be able to "capture" the object in incantation

2.   For "white," see § 14. For "foliage," see § 38.
3.   No one can face the object in its essential barrenness. But romantic poets and philosophers remove themselves from reality (the common fields) altogether:
> Far in the woods they sang their unreal songs,
> Secure. It was difficult to sing in face
> Of the object. The singers had to avert themselves
> Or else avert the object. Deep in the woods
> They sang of summer in the common fields. (C.P. 376)

in poems, the "stratagems of the spirit" (VIII). This will to make the poem, this desire for order, does not destroy the negating self which is part of the totality of the mind. The mind fashions everything, because it has to.

> The trumpet supposes that
> A mind exists, aware of division, aware
> Of its cry as clarion, its diction's way
> As that of a personage in a multitude:
> Man's mind grown venerable in the unreal. (C.P. 377)

The trumpet prophesies a new poetry based on the real, a poetry of disbelief in its own myths. But why does it *"suppose"* that a mind exists? Is Stevens calling into question the reality of the mind? Or is he saying, as seems to me more likely, that the poet realizes that the disparate halves of the mind will never be reconciled, that the mind knows full well that the poem is unreal, and deals with "Major Man," not real men, with *dichtung* not *wahrheit,* but that only one part of the mind is satisfied that this is so. The awareness of division in man's mind, and the impossibility of a final unity of vision, are what is being rendered in this poem.

The cock of reality (see § 19) looks with one eye on the modern chaos (the remains of a complex of emotions, an arrangement that has fallen apart), and with the other eye on a complex to come, when there will be made new poems of the real, poems which will not simply repeat what man wants to hear ("not part of the listener's own sense," C.P. 377.) For the "personae of summer [objects] play the characters of an inhuman author [reality]." They do not speak, except in words (characters) of the human poet in his imaginative moments beyond evil and desire ("free, for a moment, from malice and sudden cry"). The objects of reality (the basic slate) are mottled by the "red" color of reality, and, most importantly, by the "blue" of the imagination. They become complete, these meaningless unrelated objects, only in the "huge decorum, the manner of the [transient] time," the imaginative mundo.

Chapter Eleven

Notes Toward a Supreme Fiction

The first idea is an imagined thing.
The pensive giant prone in violet space
May be the MacCullough, an expedient,

Logos and logic, crystal hypothesis,
Incipit and a form to speak the word
And every latent double in the word,

Beau linguist. But the MacCullough is MacCullough.
It does not follow that major man is man. (C.P. 387)

§ 65   MacCullough, up in the air, floating in space, is a
false projection of man, a "false giant" (see § 42), part of the
process of apotheosis carried on by romantic transcendentalists. Apotheosis (the "romantic intoning, the declaimed
clairvoyance"), is one way to establish an ordered universe,
to compose a "castle-fortress-home" of permanence. One
has only to hypothesize a "MacCullough," a prime mover
who resolves all paradoxes, promises fulfillment to desire,
makes single every apparent "latent double" in his "holy
word" and in the world he is supposed to have created. But
this MacCullough, this idea about "first things," this formulation or explanation of existence, of the being of being, is
an imagined thing. The Idea of the Sun (knowledge about
the existence of material reality) is inconceivable. All god-

heads are expedients. No less so is Major Man, the fictive god of imaginative mundos. We have discussed the Major Man earlier (§ 42), and have seen that, for Stevens, he is a figure for the sum total, including the potential, of man's imaginings. Major Man is *not* MacCullough, some transcendentalist's god made in his own image.[1] Better if MacCullough immersed himself in reality, lay by the chaotic "sea" (§ 45), rather than project himself or his conception of an anthropomorphic deity up into violet space. He might learn then that there is no language, no form that will truly bind every latent double in the word, or in the world, or in the mind (the "veritable" ocean's sound is meaningless).

There are moments of feeling, to be sure, when all tensions and all double attitudes are reconciled. "Notes Toward a Supreme Fiction" is, in part, about these "moments." But it is also about the tensions and the double attitudes. The poem is finally a poem about desperation and about chaos, though not necessarily a chaotic poem.

R. P. Blackmur sees the poems as fragmentary and unsure, and in places incommunicative:[2]

He has been contented or been able only to make all his definitions out of fragments of the actual, seeing the fragments as transformations of the abstract: each one as good, as meaningful, as another, but bound not to each other in career but only to the

1. There is only critical conjecture on why Stevens uses this name, or, for that matter, many of the names he does use. I, myself, am confident that each name is carefully chosen. For example, "Mr. Homburg" (see § 7) and "Canon Aspirin." "MacCullough," however, escapes me, but his function in context is clear nevertheless.
2. See Bibliography, under Blackmur. See also Kermode. Frank Doggett's article in *E.L.H.*, Sept. 1961, sketches in the philosophic background. Glauco Cambon's article in *Studi Americani*, Vol. One, p. 205, is impressive, but he sees the doctrinal Stevens as the whole poet.

center (the major idea) which includes them. That is why, I think, so many of the fragments are unavailable except in passing, and the comprehension of what is passing depends too often upon special knowledge of fashion and gibberish in vocabulary and idiom.

I agree with the statement in the main, but important qualifications need to be made about it. It is true that all Stevens can make out of the world is fragments, parts, moments of order and beauty, but he is, in his finer poems, honest about his situation and about the necessary evasions, illusions and disillusionments, the pathos and consolations, of his psychic life with his interior paramour. As for the comprehension of the passing fragments, the special vocabulary and idiom, it is my hope that the explications of figures and postures that I have to offer, based on the anatomies that I have made, will clear up some confusions for which Stevens ought not to be held accountable. Many of the fragments seem unavailable because Stevens' attitude toward what he is saying is characteristically double, a doubleness which in places is rendered so subtly (tenuously?) that logical, consistent meaning is hard to elicit. What I propose to do here is to establish the equivocal tonalities of the various poems that make up the whole in order to provide a more solid base for judgments of the poem as a whole.

I do not want, myself, to indulge in the elaboration of ingenious schemes to prove either the absolute unity or serious disunity of this long poem. Discussions of this sort are usually remarkable for what they evade, rather than what they prove. But a few general remarks concerning the poem as a whole may be in order before a consideration of each of the parts.

The subtitles of the poem—"It Must Be Abstract," "It Must Change," "It Must Give Pleasure"—have disturbed readers. The first seems to contradict things Stevens says elsewhere, and the third seems somehow ignoble. However, after one considers the range of what Stevens is asserting in each of the three sections, it is clear that all three titles have the double meaning that is characteristic of the imaginative vision in Stevens.

Mr. Kermode admirably defines one meaning of "abstract":

> By "abstraction," as we have seen, Stevens does not mean the falsification of intellect, described in "Landscape with Boat." Blake's "minute particulars" are of the essence of his "abstract." They have to be abstracted from all the dead formulae that obscure them, to be looked on as a reality free of imaginative (or, since they are obsolete, imaginary) accretions; to be seen absolutely, "without evasion by a single metaphor." (p. 112)

But this definition hardly suffices to explain the use of the word in a central passage such as this:

> The major abstraction is the idea of man
> And major man is its exponent, abler
> In the abstract than in his singular,
>
> More fecund as principle than particle.   (C.P. 388)

"Abstraction" here is a process of selection from reality of "particles" to be "bent" to form a principle. But this is not a "falsification of the intellect" since the poet is conscious of his fabrication, it is a falsification of the imagination, a process which lends meaning to life. What the passage is saying is that the greatest feat of the imagination (the major abstraction) is the acceptance of the limitations of the mind (the inconceivability of the Idea of the Sun), and the willing repose in the Idea of Man: man not as decaying, frustrated animal, but as creator of imaginative mundos. Major Man figures the sum total of these mundos, and therefore serves as "exponent " ("proclaimer," and also "highest example") for this doctrine of the imaginative life as value. The single, particular poem, the solitary abstraction, may not last, the process of the imagination, figured as Major Man, will.

"It Must Change" does not mean simply that a particular imaginative integration (like past feelings for General Du Puy in Part II) must be discarded in time. It means also that the real, the "casual" particulars of perception must be "changed," "tipped," "curved," "bent" to form a fictive world that the will can bear:

> The west wind was the music, the motion, the force
> To which the swans curveted, a will to change,
> A will to make iris frettings on the blank.
>
> There was a will to change, a necessitous
> And present way, a presentation, a kind
> Of volatile world, too constant to be denied,
>
> The eye of a vagabond in metaphor
> That catches our own. The casual is not
> Enough. The freshness of transformation is
>
> The freshness of a world.   (C.P. 397-8)[3]

We must catch on to evasive metaphors to transform the world to our liking. Metaphor, in our time, carries with it no belief; like us, it is vagabond. Analogic fallacy has been stripped from metaphor; values outside of the ones we make have been stripped from us. (The vagabond condition of both metaphor and men is constantly reiterated, pondered in this poem.)

3.   For the first 3 lines of this passage, see § 43.

When, finally, Stevens asserts that "It Must Give Pleasure," he is not speaking as a simple hedonist who rejects the facts of reality for an oblivion of sensuality (though he does accept a life of constant, though conscious illusion). As a sober sorrowing burgher, Stevens is aware that reason and "unvarnished" perception cannot give pleasure, can give nothing like satisfaction to human desire. And so it is that the poet must accept the pleasures of evasions implicit in seeing man, in his poverty, as, say, a captain, and reality, in its blankness, as a maiden. These are transformations made, not simply for pleasure, but from a will to self-preservation:

> Each must the other take not for his high,
> His puissant front nor for her subtle sound,
>
> The shoo-shoo-shoo of secret cymbals round.
> Each must the other take as sign, short sign
> To stop the whirlwind, balk the elements.   (C.P. 401)

There is implicit in the passage a reluctance to make this desperate marriage. One would rather retain the old coupling: man (in all his nobility) with an ordered benevolent universe. The marriage, like all marriages in Stevens (§ 22), is bittersweet.

All the themes handled in the poem are bittersweet. There is praise and blame for metaphor, analogy, the will, the ego, nominalism, aesthetic formulations and orders. There is that rational destructive self in Stevens that sees so well the limitations of the mind and perception, and disbelieves in all formulations (rational or imaginative), all relationships, all analogies, and sees life as a constant war between the will, its desires, and the "blank." This war is fought in every poem, and so a natural form for Stevens is that of variation. Part II, "It Must Change," it seems to me, is wholly composed of such variations, each variation fighting some new battle in the war. Part I is a more coherent set of variations, all revolving around thoughts about the "First Idea." Part III carries through, in Sections I, III, V–IX, a fine, progressive argument concerning religious belief in the past, and a new, rather sad, religion of the imagination. Sections II, IV and X develop variations on the pleasure theme using totally different figures. Any further observations concerning form in the poem will come, perhaps, incidentally out of our own "notes" toward an understanding of the underlying emotions which impel certain passages in the poem.

§ 66 The invocation to the poem (C.P. 380) is one of the saddest things in modern poetry. I do not mean sad, grieving, but sad in its bleak vision of human poverty. It is another invocation to the Interior Paramour. The extremest book of the wisest man is the book of reality, the only one worth reading. It makes a mockery of human love and desire for permanence. The "single certain truth," the clarity that comes in uncertain moments to the poet, is that there is no truth, save that personal psychic truth in the moments of imaginative peace.

> It was when I said,
> "There is no such thing as the truth,"
> That the grapes seemed fatter.
> The fox ran out of his hole. (C.P. 203)

IT MUST BE ABSTRACT

(I–II)

One can *perceive* the objects of reality, one cannot *conceive* of how they got there. All the senses can do is perceive;

the mind, never at rest, reasons or imagines about the data collected by perception, so that the world of exterior things is, for us, always an "invented world." We abstract the moment we open our eyes, and all we know is that part of reality that we have abstracted. But the hunger is to know more, to know something about "first things," the first idea:

> It is the celestial ennui of apartments
> That sends us back to the first idea, the quick
> Of this invention; and yet so poisonous
>
> Are the ravishments of truth, so fatal to
> The truth itself, the first idea becomes
> The hermit in a poet's metaphors,
>
> Who comes and goes and comes and goes all day.
> (C.P. 381)

Man can hardly bear to live with "parts," in "apartments," confined within "walls" (the limits of his mind), but he must (see § 7). He must try "to be without a description of to be" (C.P. 205), to become an "ignorant" man without conceptions or suppositions about a prime mover, to live wholly in the sun, "to be in the difficulty of what it is to be." Otherwise the ravishments of such fruitless contemplation will become a sole obsession, ever returning to impoverish the mind and close the senses. Far better, more profitable, to think of "secondary things," objects of the "sun," and the projections of these in imaginative mundos. We must not try to conceive the idea of the sun, but to see the sun (objects) in (within) the idea of it, to focus on the objects, the "parts":

> The latest freed man rose at six and sat
> On the edge of his bed. He said,
>   'I suppose there is

A doctrine to this landscape. Yet, having just
Escaped from the truth, the morning is color and mist,
Which is enough: the moment's rain and sea,
The moment's sun (the strong man vaguely seen),
Overtaking the doctrine of this landscape. Of him
And of his works, I am sure.' (C.P. 204)

The passage demonstrates that at the very moment of seeing
the world within its idea, the mind must still project the
whole (which it cannot know) in a figure of Major Man (the
"strong man"). Phoebus, the sun god, is dead; belief in gods
is dead, but projections (imaginings) of ordering figures come
from the will, and the process cannot die. "There was a
project for the sun and is" (C.P. 381). "Project" is ambiguous
(a prime example of R. P. Blackmur's observation that
Stevens' poems are often "intentionally ambiguous at their
crucial points"). It means, in part, that there is a *"raison
d'etre"* for the "sun" (implying, one would suppose, some
sort of supernatural projector). It also means that there are
satisfactory imaginative "projections" for inexplicable
reality that the poet can project ("throw out") though not
believe in. The two meanings are compatible here since the
first merely postulates a theoretical order to reality about
which we can know nothing. (The word play throughout
"Notes" demands close attention. For example, in Section I,
a god-concept is figured as a "voluminous master." Implicit
in the figure is not only a giant beyond the height of Major
Man, but also, a giant who is master of the "book" of reality,
Stevens' favorite "volume." In Section II the young poet who
reads the book is called "prodigious scholar" because he is
studying "prodigies," a false giant, the voluminous master,
and a true giant, Major Man).

III.

Priests (monastic men) and philosophers study false giants, and their projections are but desired imaginings, just like those of the artist, except that they continue to believe in their projections while the artist then seeks for new ravishments of a new spring. His "moments" and his "pluralism" (his mundo) must be the substitute for the priest's belief in an absolute, single truth, the "monism" of the monastic man. The poet's ultimate belief is in the blank, "immaculate beginning" (without stain) and "immaculate end" (nothingness). This non-belief can suffice in those moments of the integration of feelings in an ordered poem:

> We move between these points:
> From that every-early candor to its late plural
>
> And the candor of them is the strong exhilaration
> Of what we feel from what we think, of thought
> Beating in the heart, as if blood newly came,
>
> An elixir, an excitation, a pure power.
> The poem, through candor, brings back a power again
> That gives a candid kind to everything.   (C.P. 382)

'Candor" is perfectly chosen. It means "white" and also clear, frank, honest. The ever-early candor is at once the whiteness, blankness of reality, the immaculate beginning and end of experience (see § 14), and also the honesty with which the poet accepts and works with reality. The "iris frettings" that he makes on the blank are impelled, "winged by an unconscious will" for order. The mundo so formed is the "late plural," a world of false accretions and false metaphor, yet it is honest, an end point full of candor, because the poet realizes that it is a construct of feeling and desire alone. The ravishing power of the poem is a pure power because it does not depend on the first idea to give it substance; it ravishes while still allowing for the specificity, the "candid kind" of everything, and for the unrelatedness of objects. The relations set up between objects in the mundo are "nonsense," but are strange, magical, in their power over us. For example, the poet describes the "Arabian" (a part of all of us) who thinks he can fathom the world,[4] and the wood dove who chants of his own little world, and also the ocean, which figures unfathomable jangling chaos. These three figures are not related in any fundamental way, and in fact their conjugation points their unrelatedness in phrases that delight. This is the minimum magic of poetry.

IV.

People used to think they knew, through revelation, about the first idea, the first cause. The cosmos rolled around us, we were at the centre of the diamond, God made us in his image and made the world for us. Descartes, accepting this view, declared then that the proper occupation for the mind was to study the *effects* of God's hand in our universe. The truth is, says Stevens, the only heaven is the earthly Eden and only perennial human desire fashions myths of heaven and makes necessary a Cartesian dualism. Only the ego of man sees the air and clouds as parts of a world created for it. Desire for order is compulsive in man, and is the spring of all his achievements, but it is folly nonetheless to believe,

4. I take "unscrawled fores" to mean "the way, or course, of the future that cannot be known." The Arabian is represented throwing out some devices (a fore-cast) that he believes will tell him something of the future.

or to insist, that objects bear any relation to man. (This monotonous demand of man's ego is beautifully allegorized in Part II, Section VI, in the sparrow who orders the blade of grass, "Bethou me.") The earth was a kind of paradise to the believers in the Christian myth, these sons and daughters of Eve, but they did not look at reality truly, they dwelt in a "very varnished green." For the poet who faces reality squarely in its blankness, "hard it is in spite of blazoned days," in spite of those moments of equilibrium which are embedded in "years" with the "mind in trouble" (see "Credences of Summer," C.P. 372). The air is bright or dark, the light tragic or comic as we color them in our moods, but really they and the wind are abysmal till we add our small pip of imagined meanings to them.[5]

V.

The meanings we add to the "wind" are but "sounds like pips" finally, but are roars momentarily, for they give the psyche the feeling of control over reality. The lion, the elephant and the bear press back against the pressure of reality instinctively, see their world in terms of their temporary power over it. But the poet, the young man, is self-conscious, and he sees too much:

> But you, ephebe, look from your attic window,
> Your mansard with a rented piano. You lie
>
> In silence upon your bed, you clutch the corner
> Of the pillow in your hand. You writhe and press
> A bitter utterance from your writhing, dumb,

5. For the proper feeling of "air," "light," "wind" and "cloud" in Stevens' sensibility, see chapter five on Figures of Change. For "theatre," see § 32; for "glass," see § 7.

Yet voluble dumb violence. You look
Across the roofs as sigil and as ward
And in your centre mark them and are cowed. (C.P. 384)

He looks across the roofs which are human constructions,
and sees that they are finally just more objects, wards of
reality. But the construct, the city and the civilization, are
yet marks, signs, sigil of man's creative imagination. As
another decaying animal of reality, the poet writhes on his
bed, is dumb, cowed, and bitter. But out of this bitterness
comes sweet utterance of bitter things, the poet's children,
his metaphors, which allow him to do what he will with
reality and with the violence within it. The abstracting process is all the poet has, and yet Stevens cannot help being
ironic about it. The poet lives in an attic, a mansard with
a rented piano; his metaphors warp reality, "teach bears to
juggle." The pressure of reality pushes the modern poet to
such absurdities. This section (V) well illustrates the complex attitude Stevens has toward everything he is saying. He
keeps shifting his perspective from serious to ironic, from
tragic to comic—these changes being part of the bravura
necessary to face the object.

VI.

Section VI begins with comments about the First Idea,
though it is not specifically mentioned. The section ends
with comments about the Poem. Once this is clear, the
section is much easier to read, and the transitions
are easier to follow. The essential theme is that the intense
desire for knowledge of the First Idea can only be satisfied,
in some measure, by a shunting of the imagination to
functions it can handle, to "brushings," "wettings," "roof-

ings," "virginals" and "first fruits" (metaphors), to "flick-
ings" and "bloodings." All these are evasions of the "sun"
which cannot be borne without a roof (compare "hat," § 41).[6]
The First Idea cannot be realized or named, and is not even
to be desired when the imaginative faculty is operative. But
all these statements of what one cannot do about the First
Idea carry a poignancy that suggests the deep desire of the
poet to be able to do them, a desire for more than a choice
between "false forms" and "mere air." The weather is
painted in false blues and cold whites; the forsythia as an
image gives pleasure, then passes, so does the magnolia
(compare "azaleas and so on" in "The Man on the Dump"):
the once blue, ordered sky thins to yellow, is turning "white"
(§ 14). And even the ordering "giant" (§ 42) is dissipating
into air. All real objects (the visible) were transformed by
the poet's desire (the "invisible"—compare "the physical
pine, the metaphysical pine," § 35). There is no real transformation of objects in a metaphor, but the "false flick"
has come to please:

> My house has changed a little in the sun.
> The fragrance of the magnolias comes close,
> False flick, false form, but falseness close to kin.
>
> It must be visible or invisible,
> Invisible or visible or both:
> A seeing and unseeing in the eye.
>
> The weather and the giant of the weather,
> Say the weather, the mere weather, the mere air:
> An abstraction blooded, as a man by thought.   (C.P. 385)

The passage describes the imaginative order, its objective
falseness, and the peace it brings to the subjective self. The

6. For "painting" see § 58: VI.

Major Man, or the giant, that the mind projects to fill the empty air is a fusion of desire and nothingness. "Blooding" and "abstraction" are processes looked upon by Stevens here and elsewhere with a double eye.

Now thoughts that follow a strictly logical, mathematical patterning, what Stevens calls in Sec. IX "reason's click-clack," cannot sustain us. There is another kind of thought, imaginative meditation, with the "unseeing" eye awake, that gives us figures that can sustain us at times (at "midnight"),

> He [Major Man] comes,
> Compact in invincible foils, from reason,
> Lighted at midnight by the studious eye,
> Swaddled in revery, the object of
>
> The hum of thoughts evaded in the mind,
> Hidden from other thoughts. (C.P. 387–8)

The "invincible foils" can be either the objects of reality which reason ultimately cannot handle, or metaphor, which is irrational. "From reason" is equivocal, meaning both "beginning in reason" and "escaping from it." The "studious" eye is the imaginative, unseeing eye which indulges in revery upon reality. The "hum of thoughts evaded in the mind" are, it would seem, those conjugations, metaphors, analogies, harmonies, that can be made when one is not bound to strictly logical reasoning, when the "dark-blown ceinture" is "loosened, not relinquished." (C.P. 385)

VII.

Section VII is about this second kind of thought, the imaginative meditation on reality (what some rationalists might call a deviation from "thought"). The false giant of the transcendentalists (the MacCullough) is manufactured to justify, in part, an emotional leap into apotheosis. Even the "giant of the weather" in the preceding section, that figure for the achieved poem cannot inspire the exaltation the poet feels in his imaginative moments. These moments, when ever-changing "truth" seems stable, are "moments of awakining extreme, fortuitous, personal," not achieved in the academies of thought, but occurring in walks around a "lake" (see § 7), a "stop to see hepatica," a "rest in the swags of pine trees" (see § 35) bordering the lake; they occur, that is, when one is immersed in things of the world and neither the "weather" nor the mind is in tumult. In these moments the poet does well to "stop to watch a definition growing certain" and "wait within that certainty" because once out of that moment of equilibrium ("in the centre of our being"), he will lapse back into the "uncertain light" of reality (see C.P. 380).

Stevens wonders in the last stanza of this section, and elsewhere in "Notes" whether perhaps, in these moments, "we more than awaken, sit on the edge of sleep," beyond the limits of the mind. We have seen earlier, in our discussions of the park, the portal and the foyer, that for Stevens there is no more certainty out at the boundaries of perception than in close.[7] The mind of "Canon Aspirin," later in the poem, will fly out to the edge of space, only to return to the "complicate, amassing harmony" of the world in close. However, these "irrational" moments, though they give one no lasting transcendent truth, do serve as the basis for Stevens' aesthetic and, in Part III of "Notes," serve too as a basis for a way of life. A doctrine (which admittedly smacks of wish-fulfillment)

7. See also § 5 of our introduction, where a passage is quoted that is ironic about mystic moments of timelessness, and which implies that Stevens feels his moments are no such matter.

is put forward there of a possible continuum of moments, a constant fluid coming and going from mundo to mundo, a circulation that at least keeps one from spiritual paralysis.

VIII–X.

Section VIII we have discussed in the beginning of this chapter, and the first halves of Section IX and X also have been handled above.[8] These passages deal, as we have said, with the rational, the romantic (transcendent) and the imaginative approaches to life and truth. The romantic wish for permanence (the giant prone in space) is dashed by the logical atomism (the "sea") that is all that perception can teach. The imagination alone can give an (uncertain) meaning to life by "abstracting," selecting, and "bending" particulars so that objects appear in some relation, some order, to us. The poetic process itself, the artifacts produced, and the imaginative works to come, all together are figured as Major Man. This man is precious to the dame within the poet, the interior paramour. He comes, this hero, cyclically like April or the cock bird's call and unexpectedly, as the apple falls. He is all we have left of beliefs of the past, yet he must not, cannot, be formulated, "named," or "imagined," as people of the past did their god-heads. There is nothing to see in him, really, because he is made, confected, out of our own desire (hot in our heart). So, then, if any image or visage of Major Man is to be propounded, it must be of man within reality,

8. I have neglected the handling of some details, as for instance, who Viollet le Duc is, because they are covered in the critical literature. Also, some of the specific figures have not been explicated because, in the hope of brevity and clarity of outline, I have appended an Index to Figures, to which the reader may refer. I can only hope the paraphrastic method I have adopted here does not strike the reader as evasive.

in his poverty, his old coat and pantaloons. The Rabbi, the chieftain, or the young poet (ephebe) will not find this image sanctifying, not, except in the imaginative moment, consoling, but, given the miserable human condition, he is our sole figure of victory over inanimate, difficult reality.

§ 67   IT MUST CHANGE

The poem goes from the poet's gibberish to
The gibberish of the vulgate and back again.
Does it move to and fro or is it of both

At once? Is it a luminous flittering
Or the concentration of a cloudy day?
Is there a poem that never reaches words

And one that chaffers the time away?
Is the poem both peculiar and general?
There's a meditation there, in which there seems

To be an evasion, a thing not apprehended or
Not apprehended well. Does the poet
Evade us, as in a senseless element?

Evade, this hot, dependent orator,
The spokesman at our bluntest barriers,
Exponent by a form of speech, the speaker

Of a speech only a little of the tongue?
It is the gibberish of the vulgate that he seeks.
He tries by a peculiar speech to speak

The peculiar potency of the general,
To compound the imagination's Latin with
the lingua franca et jocundissima. (IX, C.P. 396–7)

The poem is a masterpiece of equivocation. The questions, the uncertainty of the statements, are shaped so as to allow all sorts of answers and every kind of qualification. It is hardly a poetic manifesto, as some critics have tried to make it; it is rather an attempt, using some inherent ambiguities in words and language, to project in a poem about the language of poetry Stevens' double attitude toward poetry, language, and life.

"One is always writing about two things at the same time in poetry, and it is this that produces the tension characteristic of poetry." One is the "true subject" (the gibberish of the vulgate) and the other is the "poetry of the subject" (the poet's gibberish). The "vulgate," reality, the "prerogative jumble," cannot be ordered in words; it is meaningless, and hence its true representation in words would have to be meaningless gibberish. But the poem, in fact, imposes meaning and order upon reality, so that the poem is gibberish in its misrepresentation. Also, as R. P. Blackmur says, "One gibbers before a reality too great, when one is appalled with perception, when words fail though meaning persists."[9] "Gibberish" refers also to the peculiarity of the poet's form of speech, its strange analogies and syntax, so different from those of strictly logical speech, a peculiar speech which may or may not give us some general knowledge of the world. One writes about the two things, the real and the fictional; the question is whether there is any true commerce between the two save the mere sad juxtaposing of chaos and the desire for order. Is the poem simply burnished "mirror" (the concentration of a cloudy day), or a fitfully flaming "lamp" (a luminous flittering)? Does this artifact of peculiar speech give us any real knowledge about the relation between objects (one sense of "general"), does it make us understand

9. See Bibliography, Blackmur, p. 215.

better our environment and the limits of our mind ("spokesman at our bluntest barriers"), or does it merely give us
pleasure from a wholly fictitious abstraction of objects into
an imaginative mundo ("general" in a second sense)?

"Does the poet evade us, as in a senseless element?" This
is really two questions. One side of Stevens' mind, the jaundiced side, asks "Does not the poet speak nonsense through
the vehicle of evasive metaphor, fallacious analogies?" The
other side, the desperate one, asks "Is it not at least possible
that the poet gives us a knowledge beyond the facts of perception, of the 'senseless element'—information the eye
cannot gather?" But everywhere, Stevens says no to this
last question:

> "Words are not forms of a single word.
> In the sum of the parts, there are only the parts.
> The world must be measured by eye;" (C.P. 204)

The poet seeks a knowledge of reality, the gibberish of the
vulgate. And yet he is hot with a desire for the "general,"
for the "imagination's Latin," for the "poem that never
reaches words," written in a gay, honest language which can
still make some true, general statements about reality.[10] He
desires, in other words, analogy which is not gibberish. Is
there a true poem out there in reality, some order behind,
beyond? Or is that uneasiness (that misapprehension) that he
feels merely the recognition that his feelings, his desires, can
never find a harmony with reality's hum?

No answer of course is forthcoming. Much of Part II of
"Notes" is taken up with the denial of various orders that

10. "Lingua franca" is ambiguous, having the meaning of free,
unencumbered speech, but also it is a special phrase for an
Italian-Arabic jargon, a "gibberish." "Vulgate," of course,
implies both a vulgar, common language, and the language of
the Holy Book.

pretend to general truth. There is in these poems denial of even the conscious fictions of the imagination. But affirmation of them is there too. The attempt is to maintain equilibrium, to keep the equivocal tone. One eye is always fixed on the blank, while the other is making "iris frettings" on it.

(I)

The old seraph of Part II, Section I represents at once the "necessary angel of the earth" (the imagination), and also one of these angels of the old myths who joyously sniffs flowers put there by God for their pleasure. Doves in old times were not seen simply as doves, but as spirits, (like those ghosts that waft out of old books, whether chronologies or testaments). But the perfume of real life is not unqualifiedly sweet. It is "an erotic perfume, half of the body, half of an obvious acid." The sweetness is there in the world's body, if rightly imagined, but so is the acid, the acridness, in the decay of particular things. The "acid" in life is "obvious" to the right perceiver. The acid eye tells us that the booming of life in us and around us stops suddenly, is "blunt," will not resume, as the old noble mythologies promise us. What resumes, what *is* constant, is the flow of new objects, new people, new imaginings (night-blues). The holy dove returns, but under the less noble name of pigeon. A "new-come bee" takes being, not yesterday's bee with old body and heavy wing (there is a pun on "be" and "bee").

(II)

The President is a satiric figure for all the gods the transcendentalists have created; he is Stevens' anonymous-as-possible projection for the "inconceivable idea of the sun" (see § 65). In some brilliant, ironic lines of pseudo-logic, Stevens turns the tables on the transcendentalists:

> The President has apples on the table
> And barefoot servants round him, who adjust
> The curtains to a metaphysical t
>
> And the banners of the nation flutter, burst
> On the flag-poles in a red-blue dazzle, whack
> At the halyards. Why, then, when in golden fury
>
> Spring vanishes the scraps of winter, why
> Should there be a question of returning or
> Of death in memory's dream?   (C.P. 390–1)

If everything is in such perfect metaphysical order, says Stevens, if God (the President) is well served in his heaven, the country in perfect stable peace,[11] everything is nice and quiet, why, then, should we imagine upheaval where the world ends because God is dissatisfied. or the cycle of life disturbed by the resumption of life in all those that have lived? Why should we think of death as but part of a dream in the great memory? Is not the transcendentalist's imaginative myth, this "red-blue dazzle," an inconsistent one?

(III)

Section III is straightforward and needs no commenting, except, perhaps, to point out the irony with which Stevens presents the lawyers who "promenade" on Sundays, and the

11. There is an obvious pun here on the colors of the American flag, and one on the President as American leader. The transcendentalists are chauvinists.

doctors who "bathe themselves with care." The belief in the sort of nobility figured in General Du Puy is indeed vestigial in modern times, but man is shrunk now (unless heightened by the imagination) to a position of absurdity. Stevens is not easy in the past or with his peers in the present.

(IV)

Section IV is compelling in its beauty, but uncharacteristically romantic in thought:

> Two things of opposite natures seem to depend
> On one another, as a man depends
> On a woman, day on night, the imagined
>
> On the real. This is the origin of change.
> Winter and spring, cold copulars, embrace
> And forth the particulars of rapture come.   (C.P. 392)

Stevens, as we have seen in many places above, is always careful (candid) in distinguishing between the "two things" the poet writes about, the object and the poetry of the object, the odor and the acid, chaos and fictive order. The passage speaks of these two things, the imagined and the real, in figures of lovers, figures which hide the tension, the lack of a true relationship between them. The imagined depends on the real, but the real does not depend on the imaginative, except in romantic thought. It is perhaps in the rapture of the imaginative moment that we accept the first four stanzas.

Our solitude is not going to be followed by another solitude, another being; the poet's music (a "little string") speaks of this isolation and of the permanent death of multitudes.

The partakers of life, the child, the captain and the sailor, all partake of death and decay along with the poet and his companion, the imaginative self. The exhortation to "follow after" all the rest of decaying creatures is to the imaginative self ("sister and brother"), to make music of decadence; the mortal self can hardly help following. Life and death may be a pair in the cycles of the universe, but the mind of perishing man is always double, and separate. To love the beauty of life in the cycle is not to love, equally, death. The poem makes only a rhetorical reconciliation between desire and death.

(V)

The isolation of the poet (figured as a planter) and the value of his work in a larger perspective are beautifully allegorized in Section V. The planter's poems may be "garbled green," "orange blotches," to people long after, but for the poet, they are "his sea-myrtles in white sand" (flowers in the desert of the real) and his "patter of the long-sea-slushes" (an ordering of the vacuous sound of the sea). Beyond him, beyond his powers of ordering, is his aesthetic vision of a perfect order (the pineapple, see § 13), generated by desire (the phallic banana tree) and reality (the "melon," a "womb" of generation).

> There was an island beyond him on which rested,
> An island to the South, on which rested like
> A mountain, a pineapple pungent as Cuban summer.
>
> And là-bas, là-bas, the cool bananas grew,
> Hung heavily on the great banana tree,
> Which pierces clouds and bends on half the world.

He thought often of the land from which he came,
How that whole country was a melon, pink
If seen rightly and yet a possible red. (C.P. 393)[12]

"Things" are constantly being generated anew in nature; the process (the sea) keeps rolling, and we make of it what we can (on our "banjos") from out of our affective life.

(VI)

Other men who are egoists order their world without any reference to the real, but only to their desires; they see the cosmos as centered around their little "coppice" or "green glade."[13] They make a jingo heaven out of desire within them, in spite of the rain of chaos without:

There was such idiot minstrelsy in rain,
So many clappers going without bells,
That these bethous compose a heavenly gong. (C.P. 394)

The people desire without any foundation ("bell") for their wishes (clappers). Their aspirations cloud their eyes to differences in "leaves" and in "birds," and they appoint themselves episcopi (overseers) of a world without change, a world blown up out of their own will, as the glass-blower puffs up whatever he wants.

12. A feeling for the ambience of figures like "south," "cloud," "mountain," even "blue," in Stevens' mind is helpful in reading this passage. The figures Index may be consulted for citations. "Pink" is the way we see reality; we cannot see it in its essential "red," (see § 14). The phallic tree in "Le Monocle" X is similar to the banana tree in function.
13. These are variations on the "park" figure, see § 31.

(VII)

The aspirants long for an inaccessible bliss, for a paradise, for certainty, for knowledge of the first idea. The poet, in his moments (his lustres of the moon) has no need of such certainty. There are nights ("evenings" then) in "spring" when the mind is satisfied with "cloud" (§ 47). Then the real lilac suffices in itself; the poet does not mind "ignorance," and writes of the book of reality, chants of it, while knowing nothing truly about it. The poet fluctuates between moments of certain, "accessible bliss" and the long stretches of the "scholar's dark." The moments themselves are not times of transcendent knowledge, but times when the poet has more of perception in emotional equilibrium. "Fresh presentations," new fictions, come from these moments.

(X)

These presentations are "new rubbings of a glass." What we see in the glass (besides ourselves) are "local objects": the "park," the park bench, and the "lake" nearby." These "beginnings" are the poet's "catalepsy." They are what hold the poet's imagination from fantasy; he will not go beyond them in his writings. The "lake" still *is* an artificial construct of the veritable, chaotic ocean. It is full of falsifications of reality, "artificial" things. From the wind and the will are made swan-seraphs, musical tropes and "essences"—metaphors that do not exhibit the truth of things, but the truth of desire. We make ourselves, not the world, anew. We look within and fall in love with our own spirit, with the suitable amour, the interior paramour.

14. For "park," see § 31 ; for "lake" and "glass," see § 7. For lines 7–9 of Sec. 10, see § 43.

This final poem of Section II, is for Stevens the minimum statement, the most honest description of the imaginative process and product. It comes, by way of an answer, directly after the major poem (IX) which questions what the imagination really can do. Section IX in turn follows a poem of highly emotionally charged metaphor which seems to be making more than a minimum assertion for poetry. It does not really.

(VIII)

Nanzia Nunzio is a captivating figure for man's desire for order, for the beauty to be gained from reality by the "weavings" of the imaginative spirit. Ozymandias, an egoist who saw the world as centered around him, had desires (trappings with embedded "gems"), myths and beliefs that had no relation to the facts of reality. There is, Stevens asserts, really nothing in the exterior world that man's desire can "marry." One must take ultimately as lover, not even another body, but one's own desire, desire stripped of belief in "diamonds."

> I am the spouse, divested of bright gold,
> The spouse beyond emerald or amethyst,
> Beyond the burning body that I bear.
>
> I am the woman stripped more nakedly
> Than nakedness, standing before an inflexible
> Order, saying I am the contemplated spouse.
>
> Speak to me that, which spoken, will array me
> In its own only precious ornament
> Set on me the spirit's diamond coronal.
>
> Clothe me entire in the final filament. (C.P. 395-6)[15]

15. See 'drapery," § 40. For "diamond," see § 28. Nanzia Nunzio in her nakedness is to be compared with the 'Paltry Nude" (§ 51).

The poet and his interior paramour face an inflexible order of chaos and decay. Words are the only ornament to clothe desire, speech is the final answer, the spirit's diamond.

The first line of the last stanza is underpunctuated so that it is impossible to know who is speaking:

> Then Ozymandias said the spouse, the bride
> Is never naked. A fictive covering
> Weaves always glistening from the heart and mind.
>
> (C.P. 396)

I read it thus: the girl speaks and says that if one will let the imagination, the will of things, have its freedom, desire will be satisfied and the spouse will be clothed. Desire can make a trip around the world, through cold reality, and yet have her diamond coronal too. Desire is dependent only upon itself; Nanzia Nunzio does not care that all that is exterior to her is unrelated gibberish; she can live with the love of the poet's peculiar speech, which is gibberish of a different order.

§ 68   IT MUST GIVE PLEASURE

> Soldier, there is a war between the mind
> And sky, between thought and day and night. It is
> For that the poet is always in the sun,
>
> Patches the moon together in his room
> To his Virgilian cadences, up down,
> Up down. It is a war that never ends. (C.P. 407)

The poet's war is one of the mind, and its needs, against reality (sun and sky) which can give no satisfaction to desire. The "soldier's" war (§ 9) is one of the body, and its needs (its hunger for permanence), against death and decay. One battle depends on the other. The soldier's battle, the struggle for existence, is of course the poet's too. It makes a true human bond, this camaraderie in death. The soldier needs the poet, needs the sustenance of things of the spirit, the shadowy things, values, beliefs, joy in something (book or letter) even more. Night thoughts (of the imagination) must fight against day thoughts (reason). The poet is locked within reality, "in the sun," and can never transcend phenomena. He accepts this, and, in his mind (his room) he attempts by moonlight to patch a more satisfying world together. The spirit can survive with the fictions it fabricates; the body can be reconciled to such meager fare if it have no other:

> How simply the fictive hero becomes the real;
> How gladly with proper words the soldier dies,
> If he must, or lives on the bread of faithful speech.
>   (C.P. 408)

In the context of this war, Part III of "Notes" speaks of aspirations essentially religious, and of Stevens' maximum answer to these aspirations: the imaginative, irrational moment when the "fiction that results from feeling" becomes the real. It speaks of how one must try to live with this answer, of how to provoke an integration of sensations that go unprovoked in civil, rational gentlemen, and of hopes of attaining somehow a fluidity, a continuum of these moments—a state which is the supreme wish, a supreme impossibility, the Supreme Fiction.

(I)

Section I of Part III attempts to make important distinctions between the song of praise impelled by the soldier's (the multitude's, the companies') religious desire for permanence, and the hymns that come from a poet's wish to express the imaginative moment. The songs of permanence, songs of "the heart that is the common, bravest fundament" of man, are understood and sympathised with by Stevens, but not to the point of belief. Jubilas (hosanna) makes of the bleak wind and empty air a god in his holy light, a music transcending what we see.

> But the difficultest rigor is forthwith,
> On the image of what we see, to catch from that
>
> Irrational moment its unreasoning. (C.P. 398)

The poem is a more difficult construct than the prayer because it attempts, without transcendence, but by means of transforming metaphors, to convey some part of the feeling of the experienced moment. But there was no transformation of objects at that time; it is only in the poem that the poet evades reality. In the poem, the poet is a rational craftsman, reasoning about the moment "with later reason":

> We reason of these things with later reason
> And we make of what we see, what we see clearly
> And have seen, a place dependent on ourselves. (C.P. 401)

We construct in the poem, in other words, a garden, a park, a fiction about the world and our place in it, that was not part of the experience of the moment.

(II)

The moment of feeling has no words; the poem is a construct of words; we live, like the blue woman of Section II, within a nominalism that does not comprehend all of man's irrational life. Art is artificial, a blessing and an evasion. This double attitude of Stevens toward poetry makes Section II comprehensible. To speak of the blue woman (the fiction), as "linked and lacquered" is not high compliment in Stevens' vocabulary. She wears bracelets, that is, of links, relations between objects that have been imposed by a process of lacquering, putting a veneer of order over reality (compare the "very varnished green" of Eden, C.P. 383). It was "enough for her that she remembered" the feelings of the "moment," but the process of mere looking and naming (all she is left with when the moment is gone) involves rational operations and the limitations of the eye, and so "intrudes" on the clarity of the vision. Still the process is more honest than transcendence is; the woman has no wish to transcend; she does not want "feathery argentines" (a pun wherein cold silver is made into a "bird") permanently, or physical life to be less violent than it really it, or to have her summer moments imply a permanent paradise. She accepts the end of summer (abortive dream that it was), accepts cloud as cloud, accepts the inevitable stunting of physical desire and the necessary lapsing into a late, solitary, autumnal subjectiveness. There are many little shocks administered in this poem (note in context "abortive," "waste without puberty," "except for the eye") that undercut doctrinal postures. The fiction, the poem, is more than doctrine; it is a woman of two minds.

(III)

Section III is a brilliantly extended double metaphor which with little fiction parallels the world to the world under the yoke of an Old Testament God:

A lasting visage in a lasting bush,
A face of stone in an unending red,
Red-emerald, red-slitted-blue, a face of slate,

An ancient forehead hung with heavy hair.   (C.P. 400)

The poem is resolved in metaphor that figures both the poet describing the moment, and Christ describing paradise. Just as Christ "saved" the world's imagination then, the poet saves it now. Reality, unabstracted, is slate or stone (the "rock"); its color is eternally shades of red (see § 14) with small slits of "blue." Blank reality, or the Old Testament reality, is without a truly consoling myth (figured as "heavy hair," see § 26); it is a hell of red fire (flux) and choking vines. Reality, our unmerciful Jehovah, is inimical to our desires and inescapable to the eye unless the imaginative distortions of the poet color it, dress the "rock" in "flowers" (words) which have no relation to one another (no two alike). The desires of the poet and of the multitude have no relation to reality; the poet's words have no relation to things, but the poet and his words do relate to the feelings and desires of people, and this is enough.

(IV)

Man figured as a captain over reality, reality imagined as a maiden are projections of our desires, are fictions "to stop the whirlwind, balk the elements." We love reality, the truth of "things," so long as we can make of it "a place dependent on ourselves." We love the "ever hill" and the "sun" when they are married in a poem to human desire and expressed in "love's characters" (signs, or words of the world that give life to the world by the irrational marriages of metaphor).¹⁶

(V)

The stanzas following, the culminating stanzas of the poem, Sections V-X, are a pure distillation of the complex, the essential Stevens. Canon Aspirin, I feel, comes as close to a true self portrait of Stevens as we will find in the poetry. Canon Aspirin is a man of aspirations religious in nature, who has yet within him an iconoclastic self, a "headache" (compare Stevens' later dismemberment of himself into "St. John" and the "backache," C.P. 437, and § 36n). These poems are tremulous with disparate attitudes, doctrines and desires at cross purposes, pathos and sublimity, a comic and a tragic vision that do not come to a focus, but maintain the war in the human mind.

The poems, in which there is a progressive drama, open with a whimsical description of a civilized order, the sort of order Stevens enjoyed himself. But then the ordered scene is disturbed by the Canon's praise of a life (the imaginative life) that is yet not his life, or rather is not the whole story of his life.

We drank meursault, ate lobster Bombay with mango
Chutney. Then the Canon Aspirin declaimed
Of his sister, in what a sensible ecstasy
She lived in her house. (C.P. 401–2)

16. For lines 11–15 see § 65. The marriage is a desperate one of "signs" to balk the elements, but the drapery of metaphors give the effect of its being the apogee of human desire. The marriage is, after all, for a moment on the mid-day (summer) of the "year."

Stevens here practices a double distancing. He is an onlooker to the Canon's struggle, and also the interior paramour within the Canon is projected as the Canon's "sister." The sister lives in the real world, the world of "sense," as her mind (her "house") sees it, and has only her "children" (poems, the fruits of "marriage"), to make life bearable:

> The words they spoke were voices that she heard.
> She looked at them and saw them as they were
> And what she felt fought off the barest phrase. (C.P. 402)[17]

The sister does not hear angel voices, but in her moments within the real world, she has felt things that she could only "hide," or approximate, with "simple names," inadequate signs. The imaginative self within the Canon (his sister) needs only the moments of feeling; she does not need the dreams of transcendence—dreams the Canon, in another side of his being (the "burgherish" side) still clings to.

(VI)

The Canon, in Section VI, then, at "midnight," indulges in his dreams; he seeks the gold beneath the surface of the eye. The Canon (rather like Milton's Satan) investigates on imaginative wing the outermost boundaries of his park (the limitations of his mind) and then the local, familiar objects close to him (like the children). The Canon can find no ordering principle far out or in close, no foyer of the spirit, no portal at the end of the mind.[18] And so he realizes that he must limit his aspirations; his fugues, if not to be mere fanciful transcendence, must be composed within limits, within the complex of reality.

17. For the colors of the children's dress, see § 14.
18. All these figures form a cluster discussed in § 33.

(VII)

But these poems, man's "children," are temporary orders, and do not really suffice for long. They are words rationally superimposed upon the experience of a "moment" of feeling: [19]

> But to impose is not
> To discover. To discover an order as of
> A season, to discover summer and know it,
>
> To discover winter and know it well, to find,
> Not to impose, not to have reasoned at all,
> Out of nothing to have come on major weather,
>
> It is possible, possible, possible. It must
> Be possible. It must be that in time
> The real will from its crude compoundings come,
>
> Seeming, at first, a beast disgorged, unlike,
> Warmed by a desperate milk. To find the real,
> To be stripped of every fiction except one,
>
> The fiction of an absolute—Angel,
> Be silent in your luminous cloud and hear
> The luminous melody of proper sound.   (C.P. 403-4) [20]

The "moments of peace" here desired have not been experienced by the Canon, and are not the moments that man can actually have. He is desirous of too much; he wishes that "the real will from its crude compoundings come," and he wishes

19. Man fabricates orders, "buildings," "statues," but they grow "white (see § 14) with time. To expect to ever know the real is the desire of the ego, the beast within us "warmed by a desparate milk."
20. For "summer" and "winter," see § 16.

also for knowledge of the First Idea, two impossible wishes. He has here the desires of angels, and Stevens at the end of this section silences this irrepressible desire within the Canon. Moments of "discovery" are indeed possible, but they are not moments of knowledge (either of the real or of the absolute), but moments of right feeling and tranquil equilibrium. The poems about the feeling are not "meaningful," but they are "proper sound," and give proper pleasure.

(VIII)

This is the belief of Sections VIII and IX. Picture an angel with every happiness except the knowledge of the First Idea, the "golden centre," of which he has become oblivious. He once made music in his cloud of the chaos beneath, now he makes music of the real while living within it. This is the poet's position. He, the creator of the fictional angel, has the same limited pleasure.

> Is it he or is it I that experience this?
> Is it I then that keep saying there is an hour
> Filled with expressible bliss, in which I have
>
> No need, am happy, forget need's golden hand,
> Am satisfied without solacing majesty,
> And if there is an hour there is a day,
>
> There is a month, a year, there is a time
> In which majesty is a mirror of the self:
> I have not but I am and as I am, I am.   (C.P. 404–5)[21]

The poet has his "moments" of peace with his interior

---

21. For "mirror," see § 7. "Need's golden hand" is golden in that out of desire comes imaginative creations. For "hand," see § 29.

paramour, when his mind is clear of old myth and "solacing majesty." Why then can he not base a way of life on these moments, on the hope for their more constant recurrence? The poet is poor; he has nothing but what is within himself; he fills the "exterior regions" with projections of himself and his desire ("Cinderella fulfilling herself beneath the roof"). But perhaps a life of writing poems, expressions of the blissful moment, poems stripped of all else save irrational metaphor, may induce frequent moments of integration. This dialectic about a continuum of moments is perhaps not convincing to the reader, and it is apparent in the diction (the questions, the "and ifs" and "there musts") that it is not a convinced poet speaking here. The dialectic is qualified in the remaining poems.

(IX)

The moments are complete experiences; the poems about the moment are not. Stevens often makes this point, and it is made again, with great pathos, in Section IX, perhaps the most poignantly moving poem in the whole sequence. The invocation to the various birds of reality, the wren, the cock, and the robin to whistle, to bugle, to force music from reality, is really an invocation to the imaginative self within the poet to make fictions of the reality of which he is so inescapably a part. He is "in light secluded." This brilliant oxymoron suggests the mind's imprisonment and, at the same time, its enjoyment in sense perception. The poet is forced in his confines to sing for a mate, to make a marriage with local objects through the imaginative distortion of them and of his own position with relation to them. This is all he can do. He can in fact do "all that angels can" because the only angel that exists is the "necessary angel" of the earth. The imaginative faculty within the poet can make poems, ("repetitions," variations) about the poet and the object, but stops short, at all times, of attempting to conceive the First Idea. The poems so wrought, the vast number of repetitions about the phenomenological world, the sum total of man's plausible projections of himself, is figured as Major Man, no real man at all. The best poet, the "man-hero," is he that is best able to keep spinning those "eccentric" (see § 12) measures, he "that of repetition is most master." The pleasures of "merely circulating" are not the same as those inexpressible moments of feeling. They are "mere repetitions." But

> These things at least comprise
> An occupation, an exercise, a work,
>
> A thing final in itself and, therefore, good:
> One of the vast repetitions final in
> Themselves and, therefore, good, the going round
>
> And round and round, the merely going round,
> Until merely going round is a final good,
> The way wine comes at a table in a wood. (C.P. 405)

This "final good" is hardly a hedonism in Stevens. It is, in fact, the same pathetic answer as the burgher's:

> . . . in excess continual
> There is cure of sorrow (C.P. 61)

(X)

"Excess" and "final good" are the same. Out of "difference," "curved" motion, "aberration," evasion, more than natural, more than rational distortion come the fictions that result from feeling. The feeling, the moment on the gildered street at twilight, results in a rational fiction about an irrational experience. The fiction is a crude approximation of the feeling, but it is our only tangible good. Only at the moment of feeling is fluency attained, motion under control, the poet at the centre of a diamond. The moment, the "fat girl," then is held. The metaphoric evasions of the poem about the moment are something else, not the fat girl. The constant re-representation of her in poems is "an occupation, a work," a "good," because it keeps the mind in motion.

For Formulation, the mind at stasis, is the death of experience, whether the formulation be in poem or in dogma. This is so because, to Stevens, all analogy is fallacious, all vision double, all metaphor composed of disparate halves, and all "truth" but parts of an inconceivable truth. Poetry, the ever-early candor, can make us feel this tension, this dualism in all experience; what it cannot make us feel completely are the moments that come unprovoked to tell us that the world is an irrational mystery, beautiful and terrible to man and his irrational desires. The irrational in Stevens wars with the rational, self against self, and he, in all honesty, cannot reconcile the two selves. Stevens is not a poet of tranquility; tranquility comes only with "apotheosis," or in personal fortuitous moments. He is the poet of tension, the poet of irresolution, of honesty to the chaos of the mind, and the rage for order in the will.

> To speak of the whole world as metaphor
> Is still to stick to the contents of the mind
>
> And the desire to believe in a metaphor.
> It is to stick to the nicer knowledge of
> Belief, that what it believes in is not true. (C.P. 332)

Index to Figures

(reference is to § no.s)

Index of Poems Cited

(reference is to § no.'s)

Bibliography of Works Consulted

Abel, Leon: "In the Sacred Park," *Partisan Review*, XXV, pp. 86–98.

Bewley, Marius: *The Complex Fate*, London 1952, pp. 171–92.

Blackmur, R. P.: *Form and Value in Modern Poetry*, New York 1957, pp. 183–223.

Cambon, G.: "Le 'Notes Towards a Supreme Fiction'," *Studi Americani* (1955), I: pp. 205–33.

Cunningham, J. V.: "The Poetry of Wallace Stevens," *Poetry*, LXXXV (1940), pp. 149–65.

Doggett, Frank: "Wallace Stevens's Later Poetry," *E.L.H.*, XXV (1958), pp. 137–54.

—— "The Invented World," *E.L.H.*, (1961), pp. 284–299.

Ellmann, R.: "Wallace Stevens' Ice-Cream," *Kenyon Review*, XIX (1957), pp. 89–105.

Ford, Newell: "Peter Quinces' Orchestra," *M.L.N.*, LXXV, pp. 405–11.

Frankenberg, Lloyd: *Pleasure Dome*, Cambridge (Mass.) 1949, pp. 197–267.

Frye, N.: "The Realistic Oriole," *Hudson Review*, X, pp. 353–370.

Fuchs, Daniel: *The Comic Spirit of Wallace Stevens.* Duke University Press, 1963.

Heringman, B.: "Wallace Stevens: The Use of Poetry," *E.L.H.*, XVI (1949), pp. 325–36.

Howe, I.: "Another Way of Looking at the Blackbird," *New Republic*, November 4, 1957.

Jarrell, R.: *Poetry and the Age*, London 1955, pp. 124–36.

Keast, W. R.: "13 Ways Of Looking at a Blackbird," *Chicago Review*, VIII, pp. 46–83.

Kermode, Frank: *Wallace Stevens*, New York, 1961.

—— *Romantic Image*, New York, 1957.

Kreymborg, Alfred: *Our Singing Strength*, New York, 1929, pp. 500–504.

Martz, L. L.: "Wallace Stevens: The World as Meditation," *Yale Review*, XLVII (1958), pp. 517–36.

Mills, R.: "The Image of the Rock," *Accent,* Spring, 1958.

Mizener, A.: "Not in Cold Blood," *Kenyon Review,* XIII (1951), pp. 218–25.

Moore, Marianne: *Predilections,* London 1956, pp. 32–46.

Morse, S. F.: "The Native Element," *Kenyon Review,* XX (1958), pp. 446–65.

—— *Wallace Stevens: A preliminary Checklist of his published writings, 1898–1954.* New Haven 1954. (I collated the first published versions of all Stevens' poems with the final versions, using this checklist.)

O'Connor, W. Van: *The Shaping Spirit,* Chicago 1950.

Olsen, E.: "The Poetry of Wallace Stevens," *English Journal,* April 1955.

Pack, Robert: *Wallace Stevens,* New Brunswick (N.J.) 1958.

Pearce, R. H.: "Wallace Stevens: The Life of the Imagination," *P.M.L.A.,* LXVI (1951), pp. 561–82.

—— "Stevens Posthumous," *International Literary Annual,* II, London 1959, pp. 65–89.

Quinn, M. Bernadetta: *The Metamorphic Tradition in Modern Poetry,* New Brunswick (N.J.) 1955, pp. 49–83.

Ransom, John Crowe: *The World's Body,* New York 1938, pp. 55–75.

Riddel, J.: "Poet's Politics," *Modern Philology,* November 1958.

—— "Immortality as Form," *College English,* Jan. '62.

Simons, H.: "The Comedian as the Letter C," *Southern Review,* V (1940), pp. 453–68.

Stevens, Wallace: *Harmonium,* New York 1931.

—— *Ideas of Order,* New York 1936.

—— *The Man with the Blue Guitar and Other Poems,* New York 1937.

—— *Parts of a World,* New York 1951.

—— *Esthetique du Mal,* Cummington (Mass.), 1944.

—— *Transport to Summer,* New York 1947. Includes *Notes Toward a Supreme Fiction* and *Esthetique du Mal.*

—— *A Primitive Like an Orb,* New York 1948.

—— *The Auroras of Autumn,* New York 1950. Includes *A Primitive Like an Orb.*

—— *Collected Poems,* New York 1954. Includes a new section, *The Rock.*

—— *Opus Posthumous, Poems, Plays, Prose by Wallace Stevens.* Edited, with an Introduction, by Samuel French Morse, New York 1957.

—— *The Necessary Angel,* New York 1951.

Sypher, Wylie: "Connoisseur in Chaos," *Partisan Review*, XIII (1946), pp. 83–94.

Taupin, René: *L'Influence du Symbolisme Français sur la Poesie Américaine*, Paris 1929.

Tindall, W. Y.: *Wallace Stevens*, Minneapolis 1961.

Watts, H. H.: "Wallace Stevens and the Rock of Summer," *Kenyon Review*, XIV (1952), pp. 122–40.

Williams, William Carlos: *Kora in Hell*, Boston 1920.

Winters, Yvor: *In Defense of Reason*, Denver n.d., London 1960, esp. pp. 431–59.

Zabel, Morton D.: "The Harmonium of Wallace Stevens," *Poetry*, XXXIX (1931), pp. 148–54.